Battleground Europe

SOMME

BEAUMONT HAMEL
Newfoundland Park

Battleground Europe
SOMME

BEAUMONT HAMEL
Newfoundland Park

Nigel Cave

Series editor
Nigel Cave

LEO COOPER

To Stephen Austin Snr, who for many years was the
Superintendent of the Newfoundland Memorial Park and to his
wife Marcelle, who shared with him this responsibility

First published in 1994
Reprinted 1997, 2000, 2003

LEO COOPER
an imprint of
Pen Sword Books Limited
47 Church Street, Barnsley, South Yorkshire S70 2AS

ISBN 0 85052 398 2

A CIP catalogue of this book is available
from the British Library

Printed by CPI UK

For up-to-date information on other titles produced under the Leo Cooper imprint,
please telephone or write to:
Pen & Sword Books Ltd, FREEPOST, 47 Church Street
Barnsley, South Yorkshire S70 2AS
Telephone 01226 734555

CONTENTS

*Near the ruins of Hamel there is a little dwarf evergreen which some-
how hasn't been destroyed. A soldier has put a notice on it: 'Kew
Gardens. Please do not touch'.*

From a letter from John Masefield. Spring 1917
John Masefield's Letters from the Front
ed P Vansittart
Constable 1984

ACKNOWLEDGEMENTS

This book is largely the product of other men — those who wrote their accounts of the war, those who wrote Regimental and Divisional Histories, and those who wrote the War Diaries. Like other students of the Great War, I owe them an enormous debt of gratitude, providing the means as they do of making it possible to recall what happened here.

To my friends at the Commonwealth War Graves Commission I am grateful for their help in the section on the cemeteries and for finding particular graves. They have also provided some of the photographic material. I would particularly like to thank Miss Beverly Webb and Mr Jerry Gee, but also to all who help maintain the moving memorials and cemeteries that lie wherever the British or Commonwealth Soldier has fought and died.

On the Somme I have many friends and acquaintances. I would particularly like to thank M et Mme Duthois of the Hotel de la Paix in Albert, for making their hotel such a welcoming base; to Janet and Tom Fairgrieve for their warm greetings — and the coffee — at Delville Wood; to Julie and Mike Renshaw of Les Galets at Beaumont Hamel for a wonderful few days when I was doing the detailed ground work for this book; and to Steve Austin, who has succeeded his father as Superintendant of the Newfoundland Memorial Park.

I would like to take this opportunity to thank the people of the communes of: Auchonvillers; Beaumont, Beaucourt Gare and Hamel; and of Beaucourt sur Ancre, who accept the invasion of the British pilgrim, visitor and schoolchild with such phlegm and tolerate our wanderings over fields and our occasionally erratic driving. The respect that they show for our war dead and what happened so long ago is a crucial element in the atmosphere of a Somme tour.

I have received much assistance from a wide range of military museums and their curators. I appreciate all that they have done for me on the very limited budgets and resources that they have available to them. Amongst these I would like to thank a number in particular. Firstly to Colonel Scott Elliot and Mr Rod Mackenzie for the wealth of information on the 1/8th Argyll and Sutherland Highlanders that they have provided for me. I enjoyed a very productive morning working at Cameron Barracks in Inverness, and my thanks to Colonel Fairrie and his very tolerant staff (especially over the small matter of the photocopier!). For much information on the Trench Raid of 8th June 1918 I would like to thank Major Carroll of the Dorset Military Museum and Brigadier Cubiss of the Prince of Wales's Own Regiment of Yorkshire Museum. The Regimental Museums of the Tanks Corps at Bovington, the Royal Marines at Portsmouth and the Lancashire Fusiliers at Bury were willing to help in any way that they could.

Simon Clough, a pupil here at Ratcliffe, drew the maps for me, despite being in the midst of a busy GCSE year, and was tolerant of my nagging about 'getting the job done'.

Sue Cox lent me the negative of a precious aerial photograph from the war, and provided an annotated map to go with it. This loan is the product of a friendship created by a mutual interest in the Great War, and not the least enjoyable part of my interest in that conflict has been the opportunity of meeting a great array of fellow enthusiasts who have been free in sharing their expertise and knowledge as well as their convivial company. Mr George Friendship and my father, Colonel TA Cave, spent time reading through various drafts of this effort, and I am grateful to them for spotting errors; any remaining are, of course, entirely my responsibility. I would also like to thank my father for taking me to the Somme in the first place, and confirming an interest which then became an enthusiasm. I am also grateful to him and to Colonel Dick Burge and Dr Graham Keech who were on tour with me in the summer of 1993 and put up with following my needs to prepare for this book for the lion's share of our trip; thanks go to my brother, Damien, for lending us his Range Rover for the occasion, which enabled us to get to places that other cars cannot reach.

Once more pupils from Ratcliffe were diverted from the essentials of their GCSE tour to pose for photographs for this work; I hope they find their picture in here somewhere.

Finally, my thanks to all at Pen and Sword in Barnsley, in particular to Roni Wilkinson for his work in the design and production of the finished article and for his patience with wayward authors; and to John Bayne for his hospitality when I visit and to Sir Nicholas Hewitt for having the financial courage to publish my efforts.

INTRODUCTION

Beaumont Hamel is a small Picardy village, nestling in between chalk uplands and ridges north of the River Ancre. Apart from a rather rowdy time during the mid-sixteenth century French Wars of Religion, the most exciting thing that had probably happened to it was the overnight stay in its vicinity of Henry V and his rather bedraggled army as it made its way towards its glorious fate at Agincourt in 1415. Five hundred years later it featured prominently in the Somme battlefield. Yet the name does not have quite the same instantaneous evocation as perhaps Delville Wood, High Wood and Flers. The reason is that the fighting here was limited to a few titanic clashes that lasted a day or two — elsewhere on the Somme, the battles for villages and woods went on and on in a seemingly never-ending grinding action. Beaumont Hamel is therefore rather atypical of much of the Somme fighting. Yet it was to this village that I made one of the first stops on arriving in the area for my first time in August 1968, when I was fourteen. The reason? Because one battalion of the forces of the British Empire had suffered such terrible casualties on July 1st; and because that was the only battalion of the (then) Newfoundland Regiment the decision was made by its government to purchase an eighty acre site which included the bulk of the ground over which it attacked. The consequence is that they have left for posterity the finest trench park on the Western Front. When I arrived here on that summer's evening in 1968 I can remember finding remnants of tin helmets and half rusted away tins of bully beef; there was not another soul (apart from my father) in sight. The hordes come here now; but the park still retains that ability to evoke something of the past, despite the fact that all is peaceful, that sheep graze the trenches, and that the remnants of the soldiers are in the deceptive peace of war cemeteries scattered around the park.

Thus the park is the magnet that draws every first time visitor to the Somme. As time went by, and with more and more visits, I extended my interest outside its artificial boundaries and found more — much more — to interest and to admire and to grieve over. Thus the range of the book has been extended to cover the ground from Redan Ridge to the Ancre, and to give at least a cursory look at some of the villages behind the Front Lines which were home to the opposing armies.

It should be noted that, like my first book in this series, *Sanctuary Wood and Hooge*, this is not by any means meant to be an inclusive guide. Although the style is similar to that work, the battles here were of such a different character (a few pitched battles and a relatively short period of trench warfare between Briton and German compared to four years of unceasing struggle and action) that it is perforce rather different in content, with rather more factual description of what went on between the opposing forces. There is enough in it, I hope, to give a reasonable explanation as to what was going on — possibly in some cases why it was going on, but I have only been able to cover a few of the incidents and personalities that figured in the history of this place. On the other hand, I hope that it provides enough to give all readers the food for thought that this place, and the intention of the Government of Newfoundland, should provide.

'Going up to the trenches'. Passing through the village of Hamel in the autumn of 1916.
Taylor Library

ADVICE TO TOURERS

I have talked of guides and other reading in a separate section of this guide.

As regards maps, those in the guide are meant to be sufficient for the purpose of the immediate area. The Commonwealth War Graves Commission produces the standard Michelin map overprinted with details of its cemeteries; this is obtainable from 2, Marlow Road, Maidenhead, Berks SL6 7DX. The best map for navigating from is the 1:100 000 version produced by the IGN (the French equivalent of the Ordnance Survey). You want Number 4 in the Green series, titled Laon and Arras. This is available in most newsagents and bookshops in the area. There are also the Red series 1:50 000 (Bapaume for this area), and the excellent Blue series 1:25 000 (Bapaume West, but Bapaume East would be useful, as Beaumont Hamel is close to the edge of the map) available, but they are a little more difficult to come by.

I talk elsewhere of relics from the Great War. There are plenty of harmless pieces of shrapnel scattered about the place, but please do be warned of the danger from the shells, grenades and mortar bombs that are still found in considerable profusion along the old battle lines. There is no reason to treat them in any more cavalier fashion than one would with a similar find in your garden at home.

There are a number of hotels in the region. I have often stayed at the Hotel de la Paix in Albert; the proprietor is most helpful, and his wife produces an excellent meal at supper. The restaurant is popular with the locals — a sure sign of good food and value for money. There is also the Hotel Basilique in Albert, and both provide good value accommodation. There are more palatial rooms provided at the Hotel de la Paix in Bapaume, and in a large hotel on the outskirts of Rancourt. Finally, there are an increasing number of British owned Bed and Breakfasts in the area: at Ligny Thilloy at 12 Rue d'Arras, Tel 21 59 52 48; at Auchonvillers, just behind the old British Line before the Hawthorn Crater at Les Galets, Tel 22 76 28 79; also in Auchonvillers, in the village itself,

View from Malins' position across No Man's Land and the British positions. Old Beaumont Road is in the centre of the photograph.

Tel 22 76 23 66; and in Mailly Maillet, at La Maison Blanche, 24 Rue Eugene Dupre, Tel 22 76 28 65. I have stayed at the first two named here, and can vouch for the comfort of the rooms, the hospitality of the hosts and the high quality of the meals (dinner is usually available on request).

A lunchtime drink is often difficult to come by — there are not many cafes in the area. Your best bet would be to go to Albert, to Puisieux, or to an excellent little auberge on the road between Authuille and Aveluy. Should you merely want to buy a coffee and browse through an excellent range of Great War books for sale, then I would suggest you visit the South African Memorial at Delville Wood. There are also tables outside for your French-style picnic of baguette, cheese, ham and tomatoes.

There are two museums within easy access. A new one has been opened in the old Second World War air raid shelters in Albert; the entrance is alongside the famed basilica. The French have opened a most impressive 'Historial' in Peronne — it is expensive to gain entry, but is well worthwhile. Amongst other things it reminds us of the French and German armies that fought on the Somme, and of the poor civilians who suffered so much in the dark days of the Great War.

I would recommend comprehensive insurance cover of yourself and your car. Bring all medication that you are likely to need with you. Ensure that your tetanus jab is up to date. Film is expensive on the continent, as are batteries, so ensure that you have all your camera requirements. A small notebook and pen or dictaphone are helpful — very often there are things that you want to note down, or to write details of the photographs that you have taken. A pair of binoculars is also useful. A corkscrew is almost as necessary as strong walking shoes or a pair of wellingtons.

Finally, bring a sense of awe with you, for this place deserves it.

HOW TO USE THIS BOOK

The book is split into chapters which run on more or less chronological lines. The reader has a number of alternatives when using it as a guide. One is to sit somewhere and read the whole thing through in a sitting or sittings before making one's visit to the battlefield. A relevant map is usually included, where appropriate, in each chapter. References are made to other maps, where necessary, at an appropriate point in the margin.

It might be that the tourer wishes to follow the events at Beaumont Hamel chronologically — in that case simply start at the beginning, visit each area under discussion in turn, and spend a fair amount of your time driving from point to point.

Should you wish to deal with a whole area at a time, then look at Chapter 16 in the section under the walking tour. This has been split up into parts, and I have indicated which chapter is relevant to the ground being covered. There is an element of repetition of viewing instructions — usually each chapter starts by giving details of vantage points, and this is on occasion repeated in the Walking Tour instructions. It seemed, however, to be the best way to ensure that the visitor is best served by the guide.

I would recommend, if you are mobile, that you follow the car tour at the beginning of Chapter 18 to familiarise yourself with the terrain before attempting to follow things on the ground.

There is a section which gives a brief description of the cemeteries and the memorials in the area under discussion in the book.

LIST OF MAPS

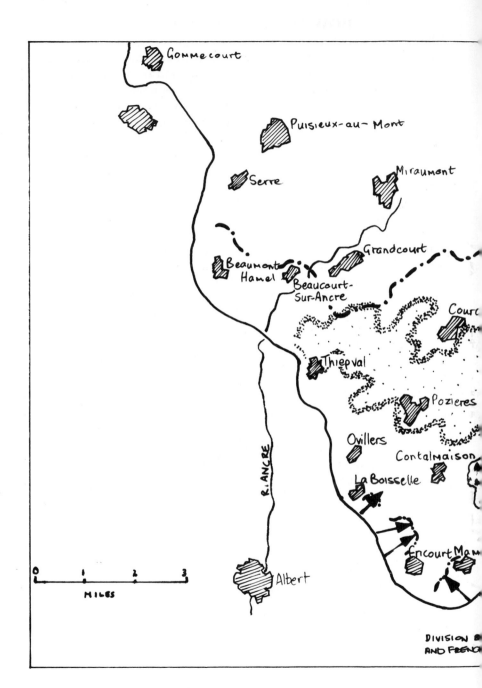

Gommecourt

Puisieux-au-Mont

Serre

Miraumont

Grandcourt

Beaumont Hamel

Beaucourt-Sur-Ancre

Courc

Thiepval

Pozieres

Ovillers

Contalmaison

La Boisselle

R. ANCRE

Encourt Man

Albert

0   1   2   3

MILES

DIVISION B
AND FREN

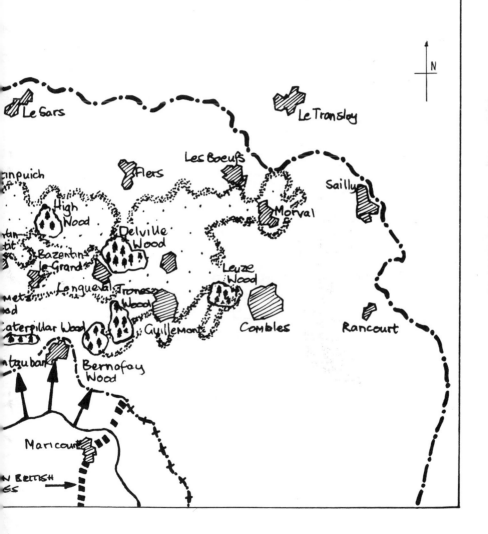

Map 1. THE BATTLE OF THE SOMME 1916

This shows the advances made on 1 July, 1916, and the final line reached by the Allies at the end of the battle.

Bapaume

N

Le Sars

Le Transley

Flers

Les Boeufs

Sailly

inpuich

High Wood

Morval

Bazentin le Grand

Delville Wood

Leuze Wood

Longueval

Tronos Wood

Guillemont

Combles

Rancourt

Caterpillar Wood

tzuba

Bernafay Wood

Maricourt

BRITISH

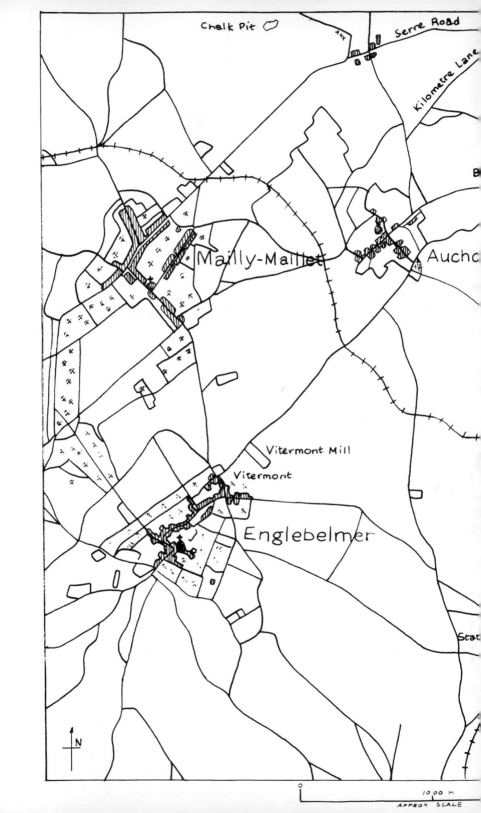

Chalk Pit

Serre Road

Kilometre Lane

Mailly-Maillet

Aucho

B

Vitermont Mill

Vitermont

Englebelmer

Stat

N

0   1000 M

APPROX SCALE

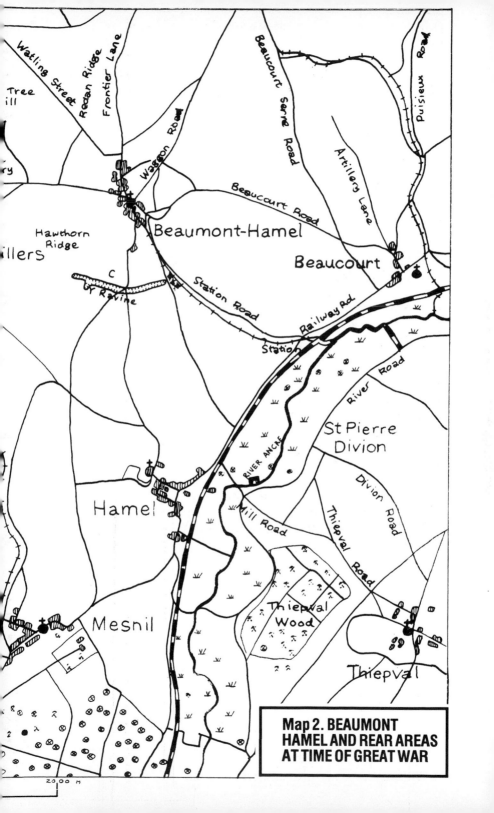

Watling Street
Redan Ridge
Frontier Lane
Tree
ill
ry
Waggon Road
Beaucourt Serre Road
Puisieux Road
Artillery Lane
Beaucourt Road
Hawthorn Ridge
Beaumont-Hamel
Beaucourt
illers
C
Y Ravine
Station Road
Railway Rd.
Station
River Road
River Ance
St Pierre Divion
Divion Road
Hamel
Mill Road
Thiepval Road
Mesnil
Thiepval Wood
Thiepval

Map 2. BEAUMONT HAMEL AND REAR AREAS AT TIME OF GREAT WAR

20.00 M

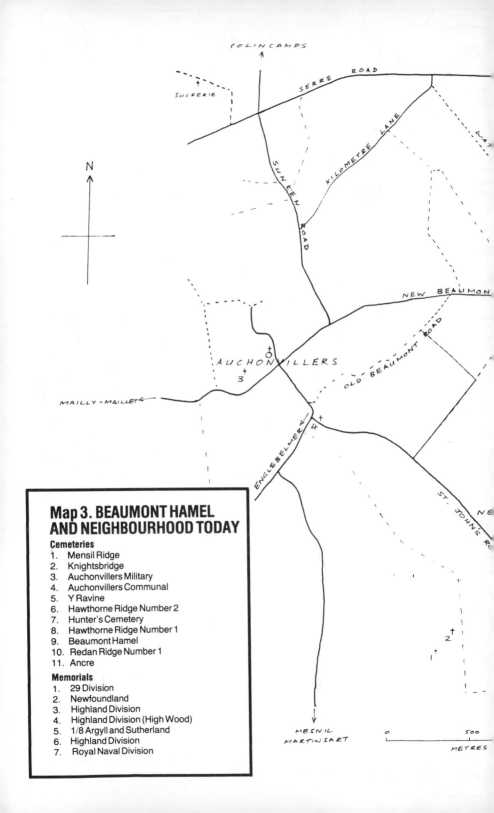

COLINCAMPS

SERRE ROAD

SUCRERIE

SUNKEN ROAD

KILOMETRE LANE

WAY

N

NEW BEAUMON

AUCHONVILLERS

OLD BEAUMONT ROAD

3

MAILLY-MAILLET

ENGLEBELMER

4

ST. JOHN'S RO

NE

NE

2

MESNIL
MARTINSART

Map 3. BEAUMONT HAMEL AND NEIGHBOURHOOD TODAY

Cemeteries
1. Mensil Ridge
2. Knightsbridge
3. Auchonvillers Military
4. Auchonvillers Communal
5. Y Ravine
6. Hawthorne Ridge Number 2
7. Hunter's Cemetery
8. Hawthorne Ridge Number 1
9. Beaumont Hamel
10. Redan Ridge Number 1
11. Ancre

Memorials
1. 29 Division
2. Newfoundland
3. Highland Division
4. Highland Division (High Wood)
5. 1/8 Argyll and Sutherland
6. Highland Division
7. Royal Naval Division

0   500

METRES

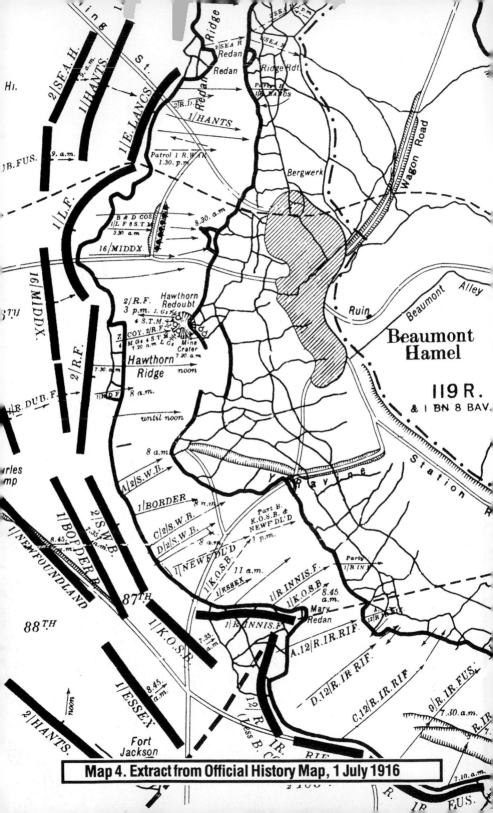

Map 4. Extract from Official History Map, 1 July 1916

BEAUMONT HAMEL AND THE FIRST DAY OF THE SOMME

This is a brief note to give some indication as to what happened on July 1st 1916 between the north bank of the River Ancre and the Redan Ridge, which rises to the north above Beaumont Hamel. **See Map 4**

The boundary between X Corps to the south and VIII Corps to the north went through Mary Redan eastwards towards Beaucourt Station, and then followed the route of the railway line. This same boundary marked the divide between the 'Incomparable' (the name they had given themselves at Gallipoli) 29th Division and the 36th (Ulster) Division. The task of the two battalions from the 36th Division attacking north of the Ancre was to secure the ground between Mary Redan and Beaucourt Station and to establish a number of defensive points on the western rise overlooking Station Road; they were also to occupy the station, the mill and a couple of houses beyond the station. The right hand battalion was the 9/Irish Fusiliers, which managed to get some of its men close to Beaucourt Station, having succeeded in breaking through the German front line trenches. To the left of the attack, 12/Irish Rifles found that the wire, at this point quite well concealed from direct view by the British as it lay over the crest of a hill, had not been well cut. What gaps that existed in it were covered by German machine gun fire, and no one could get through on the initial assault. A couple of subsequent attacks by hastily reorganised men from the battalion failed — not only did they have the machine

German front line trench at Beaumont Hamel manned by men of 119 Infantrie Regiment.   *Taylor Library*

guns still to contend with, but they had lost the supporting British barrage. The attack fizzled out rapidly, and by 8 am the Germans had retaken their original front line positions.

The 29th Division, to their left, was fated not even to have the support of an artillery barrage at zero, 7.30 am. The decision to fire the Hawthorn Redoubt mine early, at 7.20 am, is discussed in full later; for reasons that will forever remain unclear, all the field howitzers on the whole of the Corps front were ordered to lift from front line machine gun positions at that time. This was almost certainly an administrative error — the purpose of the instruction was to enable men to get close to the mine so that they could occupy the crater quickly when it blew. Matters were made even worse by orders to the divisional field artillery to redirect half their firepower to the Support Line three minutes before zero. The onslaught at the great moment, zero hour, on 29th Division front, at least, was going to be a very strange affair — as far as the artillery was concerned, zero was to all intents and purposes zero minus ten.

To compound the problems of 29th Division there also lay the strength of the German position at Beaumont Hamel. They had built a veritable fortress out of the topographical advantages that it enjoyed. From the far side of the River Ancre it came under protective fire and artillery observation from the Schwaben Redoubt — just stand by the Ulster Tower and look across today and see the view that these Germans had. Behind Beaumont Hamel the German defences ran like a grandstand on the forward slopes, up to the Second Line in the area of the Beaucourt Road — a view which may best be appreciated to-day from the neighbourhood of Frankfurt Trench Cemetery. Beaumont Hamel itself was protected by Redan and Hawthorn Ridge and the natural declivity that is Y Ravine (Leiling Schlucht to the Germans). The Germans had had months to make full use of the chalky ground to construct strong points, dug outs and complex tunnel systems. It would require massive firepower to overcome these defences.

This was something the British did not have, though it is no part of this account to describe the failures of munitions production. There was a shortage of the heavy howitzer whose shells had the best chance of busting these fortifications; what ones there were suffered from very poor quality shells — either because the fuse failed, or even fell off in flight! In short, the success of the attack of the 29th Division probably depended more on a prayer than any other point on the Somme front — and that is saying something,

Men of the Middlesex Regiment retreating from before the crater on Hawthorne Ridge – 7.45 am on 1 July 1916.

given the formidable task that faced the British Army on that day.

The battle commenced, the various battalions moved to the attack, and the attack crumpled. The Germans were alerted by the blast of the mine, and were able to man their parapets with relative impunity as the shell fire largely lifted off their positions. Men from the 2/Royal Fusiliers were unable to capture the crater, and held only a tenuous grip on the westernmost edge, whilst survivors from the battalion used the heap of earth that it had created as a means of cover. 1/Royal Dublin Fusiliers found themselves under fire from German defenders on the ridge to the immediate north of Beaumont Hamel, whilst 1/Lancashire Fusiliers and their support, 16/Middlesex had come under withering German enfilade fire from Hawthorn Ridge as well as from their front. The attack on 86th Brigade front had come to nothing; nothing at all.

Further south the attack of 2/South Wales Borderers collapsed within five minutes of zero, succumbing to scything machine gun fire from Y Ravine. 1/Royal Inniskilling Fusiliers attacked in platoon file due to local tactical considerations (elsewhere, as is all too well known, waves of infantry in extended line was the norm). A reasonable number manged to cross the German fire trench, which seemed unoccupied; they were caught from the rear as up to a company of the enemy, who had been concealed in deep dugouts, manned their parados (that is the rear of the trench) and caught them from behind. The fighting continued for rather longer on this flank of the 87th Brigade attack

Good communications, quick and accurate, were a pipe dream for commanders in World War I. This, the desperate desire to hear good news and act on any scrap of information that might be optimistic, meant that the lull in shell fire in No Man's Land, the report from RFC contact aircraft that men in khaki had been

21

seen well beyond the German front trenches and the sight of white flares (a pre-arranged signal for British success; unfortunately also a German signal for artillery support) meant that the planned 8.05 am assault by 1/Border and 1/King's Own Scottish Borderers went ahead. It had come to a grinding halt in a blockage of dead and wounded within ten minutes. Delays in communication between Brigade and Division meant that the higher formation commander, de Lisle, ordered the attack to be continued, based on the original optimistic reports, using the rear, 88th, Brigade. The Newfoundlanders set off unsupported soon after 9 am — 1/Essex, who should have gone with them on their right, found that the heavy German shell fire on the British trenches in their sector and the clogging of the crossings of trenches even behind the British front line with dead and wounded provided massive obstacles, could only attack later, and found themselves cut down. It was the artillery observers and staff on Brock's Benefit, a position on Mesnil Ridge which enabled them to see what was going on on at least part of the battlefield, who convinced Major General de Lisle

Major General Beauvoir de Lisle. His other claim to fame is as the founder of the modern game of Polo.

that the attack had been a complete failure and who stopped 4/Worcesters and 2/Hampshires being further sacrificial victims. The attack on 87th Brigade front had come to nothing, nothing at all. It had not been a good day for the Incomparable 29th.

BEAUMONT HAMEL AND THE EARLY DAYS OF THE BATTLE OF THE ANCRE, NOVEMBER 13th 1916

The last great hope for strategic success on the Somme had come on September 15th, at the Battle of Flers-Courcelette, though this was only apparent to Rawlinson, the commander of the Fourth See Map 5 Army a week or so after that date, and not the opinion of Haig or the commander of his Reserve Army, Gough, who felt that the German army might crack at any moment with just one more push.

In due course, however, all of them turned to tactical reasons for continuing the attack in to the winter. In the case of the sector around the Ancre, the German position gave them clear views right down to Albert — go to the area of Frankfurt Trench Cemetery and the site of the Beaucourt Redoubt to see for yourself. This would be a major impediment to preparations for any offensive the British might have in mind for the spring of 1917. The continuing British advance around Thiepval and along the Albert-Bapaume road throughout September and October meant that the German position around Beaumont Hamel and St Pierre Divion found itself increasingly exposed to observation and artillery fire from the flank.

Gough's Fifth Army was tasked with capturing the Ancre heights, right up to Serre in the north and towards Pys in the east. He found its planned offensive operations stymied by the weather, and by November 13th it was a case of now or never — the attacking divisions were being worn down by fatigue, the conditions and the sea of mud. In this book I am simply concerned with the 63rd and the 51st Divisions. These two, and the 39th Division on the south side of the Ancre, were successful in gaining the bulk of their objectives; the operations of the 51st and 63rd Division are to a large extent described elsewhere. Further to the north the attacks failed, and Serre and Puisieux remained firmly in German hands until their withdrawal in the spring of 1917; Serre had the distinction of being the only front line village on the old German front of July 1st that they still retained at the end of the battle of the Somme on November 19th, when the bloody onslaught finally slithered and sank into the mud around Frankfurt Trench.

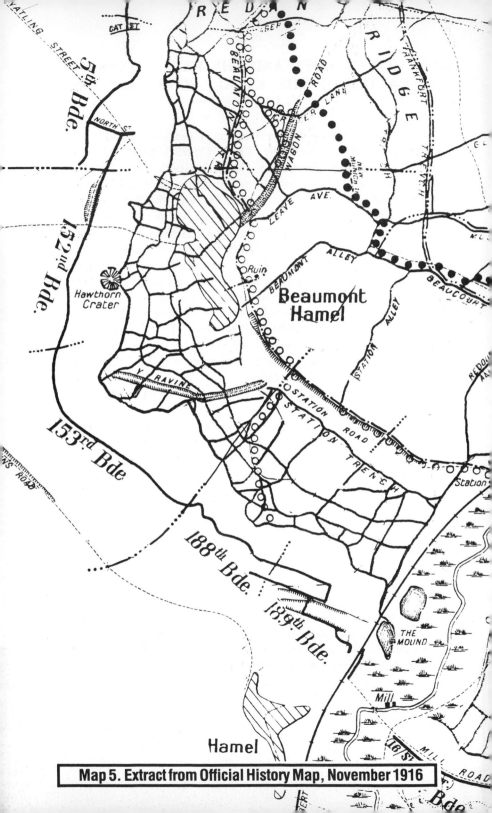

Map 5. Extract from Official History Map, November 1916

THAT FATAL MINE

*Access to the Hawthorn Crater is obtained from the Auchonvillers — Beaumont-Hamel road. The path rises very steeply from the side of the road, and is confined within a very narrow set of barbed wire fences. This path can be quite treacherous, especially when the ground is wet, and it is quite likely that you will slip, and the barbed wire may well do its worst. It is worth emphasising the point, therefore, that **you ensure that your tetanus jab is up to date!** When one reaches the end of the path, there is further fencing around the perimeter of the crater, and you have to duck and weave to make progress. The physical contortions involved are not helped by the overhanging branches and assorted thickets waiting to spring out at you. There is a path of sorts down into the crater, but it is full of undergrowth and trees and also — in my experience — remnants of shells and mortar bombs. You enter the crater very much at your own risk. However the journey up the hill is worthwhile, if only to get a better idea of the observation the Germans had over the British lines, and in particular Jacob's Ladder and the Sunken Road. An altogether more accessible viewing point is Hawthorn Ridge Cemetery No 1; this point is also handily close to the site of the shaft for the mine.*

The mine crater that is now such a prominent feature of Hawthorn Ridge because of the shrubbery and trees that have grown around and in it played a vital part in the disastrous British attack in this sector of the 29th Division attack on July 1st. But before discussing

A view of the Hawthorn Crater to-day from the rear of the Sunken Road.

the history of this crater it is worth looking briefly at the role that mine warfare played in the war in the British Army up to this date.

When the war settled down after the initial frenetic rushes, attacks and counter-attacks of 1914, both sides found themselves occupying fortified earthworks, with varying degrees of geographical domination. To help to solve local tactical problems both sides used mines to gain some advantage over the other. Some of the most brutal fighting of the war took place in the struggle to dominate the crater that was created — and indeed often in the tunnels themselves as one side or the other broke into an enemy's workings.

The British, as in so many aspects of mass warfare, were rather slower than the Germans and the French in organising specialist Tunnelling Companies, despite the fact that the huge British mining industry with both its engineering and worker expertise should have placed them on at least an equal footing with these powers. However, the companies came into existence in February 1915 when a series of reverses caused by German superiority in this particular art of warfare made their need an overwhelming necessity. The first year or so of these tunnelling companies saw them in action in the Ypres sector (where the names of The Bluff, Hill 60 and St Eloi still mean so much in this regard), in the area north of La Bassee and from the spring of 1916 in the Souchez and Vimy Ridge part of the Front.

Most of the work in this early period was of a limited, and generally defensive nature — to foil German mining by blowing camouflets. These limited charges were designed to destroy enemy galleries, or pre-empt them from blowing their own mine. Other charges were designed to provide very limited improvements to our front line positions and on rare occasions to support trench raids. The Somme gave the Tunnellers their first real chance to assist in a major offensive action.

They had a threefold purpose. Firstly the intention was to harry German mining operations and reduce them to the barest minimum. Secondly they were to prepare a number of British mines to assist the attack, generally to remove formidable German defensive positions — usually with good fields of observation, generally redoubts (miniature earthwork fortresses) and often in a position to dictate the battleground over a considerable distance. Thirdly they were to construct Russian Saps. Russian Saps were widely used during the Crimean War, hence their name. They were shallow tunnels — often only a foot or so underground — carved out

26

The horrors of working underground in the nerve-wracking business of mine warfare.

towards the enemy line. They were then opened up at the vital moment of the assault, thus providing new communication trenches as close to the German line as was practicable. These saps were especially relevant on the Somme because the distance between the two sides, No Man's Land, was often so wide — five hundred yards was not uncommon. Some of these saps had branches and complete mortar positions pre-positioned in them.

The Hawthorn Mine was designed to remove a German redoubt that protruded from the German line, and which provided them with dominating views over much of the north side of the 29th Division sector. 252 Tunnelling Company was responsible for the VIII Corps Front that stretched from Hebuterne to just above Hamel, north of the Ancre. By April they had nineteen hundred attached infantry, often making use of the mining skills available in the Pals Battalions coming into the sector, such as the Barnsley Pals. On Hawthorn Ridge there were already two defensive mines, but now the need to destroy the Hawthorn Redoubt made it necessary to prepare an offensive mine, dug from a shaft near Pilk Street, and known as H.3 (the defensive mines were H.1 and H.2). It was seventy five feet deep, and headed almost directly for the German strongpoint some three hundred metres away. *The Tunnellers*, a history of the Tunnelling Companies, goes on to describe their efforts, "By the end of May the gallery had been driven out over nine hundred feet, and was giving considerable trouble on account of the hardness of the chalk and the large

See Map 6

amount of flints in the face. From this point (ie only one hundred and fifty feet from the enemy) it was essential that the work should proceed silently and, in order to facilitate this, the face was drenched with water to soften it, and the chalk and flint prised out with a bayonet, the lumps being caught by the hand to prevent them falling on to the floor with a thud, and so disclosing our position. In due course the drive reached its objective, and a chamber was constructed; into this was loaded a charge of 40,600 pounds of ammonal (it would take six three ton lorries to carry that now); all was in readiness for Zero."

The charge was a considerable one; it was what is termed an 'overcharged' mine; that is, more explosive than was necessary to blow the mine was put in to create a greater output of earth, and thus a bigger crater lip. In this case the lip was eighteen feet above the old ground level, and thereby created a new breastwork for the infantry and protected them from enfilading (fire from the side) fire.

The question that exercised the minds of VIII Corps Headquarters was the timing of the detonation of the mine. Lieutenant General Sir Aylmer Hunter-Weston (nicknamed Hunter-Bunter) wanted to fire it some four hours before zero, thereby enabling the crater to be captured and consolidated before the general attack, but also to allow initial German alarm to calm down before the main assault at 7.30 am. This suggestion was vetoed by GHQ. The Inspector of Mines argued against the plan on the basis that the British had not yet 'made a good show' at occupying a crater; the Germans on the other hand were experts in the art. Eventually a compromise was reached that the mine should be fired ten minutes before the attack, which was

The Hawthorn Redoubt mine erupts, 7.20 am 1 July, 1916.

transparently of little value to anyone, except perhaps to some on the 29th Division staff, who felt that if the mine was fired at the time of the attack that the advancing infantry might be hit by descending debris — a fear which was relatively groundless, as previous experience on other fronts had shown. Not only did the mine give a clear warning to the Germans, but because of the associated rush to occupy the crater by the British, the Heavy Artillery was ordered to lift off the front line on the whole of the 29th Division front at that time — as well as a good deal of the 18 pounder field artillery. Thus the Germans coming out of their dugouts were able to occupy their trenches with relative impunity.

The blast destroyed the redoubt, blew up several sections of German infantry, and stove in several large dugouts, entombing a number of occupants. But it was a tactically catastrophic event on this sector's front, and the consequences to the men attacking in the Sunken Road and further south towards the edge of Y Ravine may be readily appreciated by standing on the perimeter of the crater. The Germans were already undoubtedly aware of the imminence of the British attack — the obvious lanes (and these were too few and led to bunching) in the British wire was as clear a signal as any. What it did was also to allow them almost unhindered occupation of their main trenches without the fear of artillery fire — and for several minutes before the actual attack proper. The 2/Royal Fusiliers and 16/Middlesex, the battalions attacking this particular area, were to suffer 561 and 549 casualties respectively; there would have been about 800 of them involved in each battalion in the attack.

The German Regiment on Hawthorn Ridge gives this account of the early moments of the attack. "During the intense bombardment there was a teriffic explosion which for the moment completely drowned the thunder of the artillery. A great cloud of smoke rose up from the trenches of No. 9 Company, followed by a tremendous shower of stones, which seemed to fall from the sky

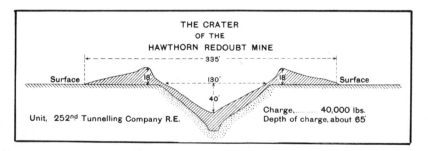

THE CRATER
OF THE
HAWTHORN REDOUBT MINE
335'
Surface 18 130' 18 Surface
40'
Charge, 40,000 lbs.
Unit, 252nd Tunnelling Company R.E.
Depth of charge, about 65'

29

over all our position. More than three sections of No. 9 Company were blown into the air, and the neighbouring dugouts were broken in and blocked. The ground all round was white with the debris of chalk as if it had been snowing, and a gigantic crater, over fifty yards in diameter and some sixty feet deep gaped like an open wound in the side of the hill. This explosion was the signal for the infantry attack, and everybody got ready and stood on the lower steps of the dugouts, and we rushed up the steps and out into the crater positions. Ahead of us wave after wave of British troops were crawling out of their trenches and coming forward towards us at a walk, their bayonets glistening in the sun."

John Masefield wrote a memorable account of a progress along the Somme battlefront, *The Old Front Line*, in 1917. At the end of March 1917 he wrote of the crater, ". . .we saw the immense and awful crater of Beaumont, which is one hundred yards long, twenty deep and fifty across, but though it is very terrible, it is less imposing than the Boiselle one, because it is not one vast white hole, but streaky, red and white, and so looks like a butcher's shop instead of an immense white sepulchre."

The front at Beaumont Hamel remained stable until the death throes of the Battle of the Somme in November 1916. Then the crater was to have the notable distinction of being fired again. The decision to reopen existing workings was not greeted with enormous enthusiasm, as the Germans should have been well aware of what had gone on; however, the old H.3 Gallery was reopened, and was made usable for some distance until the old tunnel was found to be crushed because of the July 1st explosion. A branch was

'... the immense and awful crater of Beaumont ...' Hawthorn Crater in early 1917.

made and a chamber excavated which used 30,000 pounds of explosive. A number of new saps were constructed from trenches on both sides of the Beaumont Road — from North, Hunter and South Streets and Beaumont.

The Germans were not idle — they fired camouflets, and two soldiers who went into the gallery to investigate, without the benefit of their 'Proto' apparatus (a primitive oxygen mask and cylinder system) were killed by gas poisoning. The British had even more grandiose plans; a great new tunnel was projected, nicknamed the Great Eastern Tunnel, which would go at depth of one hundred and eighty feet under Beaumont Hamel itself, with the shaft at White City. The time factor (it was thought that it would take six months to construct it) put paid to that idea. Besides firing camouflets, the Germans also kept up a heavy barrage, but despite this, and the occasional entombment of soldiers under ground when entrances got blown in (such as occurred in First Avenue Tunnel, all eventually rescued), the mines and saps were maintained.

The second firing of the Hawthorn Mine succeeded in breaking into the old crater, destroying most of its occupants, and the debris was such that it caused considerable damage to the neighbouring German trenches and dugouts. This second firing was to be the prelude to an altogther happier result for British arms which will be considered later in this book. That this is a double crater is just about perceptible when one gets to the bottom of today's silent but eloquent reminder of the efforts of the Tunnelling Companies.

(*Over the page*) **British troops in a ditch which served as a communication trench during the preliminary bombardment prior to the attack on Beaumont Hamel, 1 July 1916.**

LANCASHIRE FUSILIERS — IN THE LINE AND OVER THE TOP

The ground over which the Lancashire Fusiliers operated on and around July 1st is open to public access, but is not easily covered by car. The best option is to leave the vehicle next to the 1/8 Argyll and Sutherland Highlanders' Memorial in the Sunken Road and then proceed by foot along the various tracks. Stout shoes are essential. Good viewing points of the British line may be had from the vicinity of the Bowery. The German view point is most easily seen from the area of Hawthorn Ridge Cemetery Number 1, though it should be remembered that this is some yards in front of the original German Front Line. The view from the north side of Hawthorn Crater graphically underlines the exposed nature of the Lancashire Fusiliers advance. There are traces of dugouts and possible Stokes Mortar emplacements in the bank of the sunken road facing the Germans. Following the Sunken Road to its northern extremity will bring you beyond the 29th/4th Divisional boundary, and the point from which the 8.15 am assault was made, and to Redan Ridge Number 2 British cemetery, which was fifty yards or so in front of the German Front Line on 1 July, 1916.

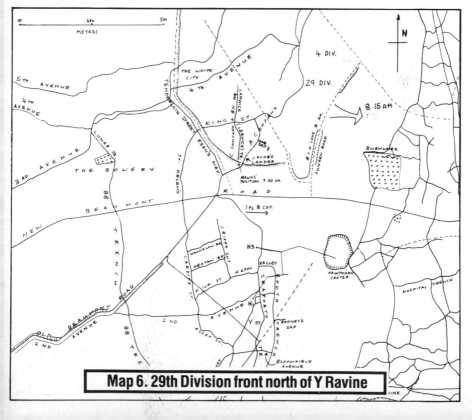

Map 6. 29th Division front north of Y Ravine

The Lancashire Fusiliers arrived in Mailley Maillet in the early days of April 1916, having landed at Marseilles on the 20th March. They were to occupy a particularly awkward part of the line, which ran in a convex semi-circle from White City to the southern side of the New Beaumont Road. Their trenches were in a bad way, the parapets being far from bullet proof, whilst the communications trenches were often in a disastrous state. It was bad enough that the Germans had numerous points from which the bulk of the position could be overlooked; for such insecure access routes had to be improved rapidly. Not only the trenches were a problem. The 29th Division had lost eleven hundred officers at Gallipoli, and there was obviously a great need to train the new ones up to a state of efficiency. The comparative professionalism of the opposing forces was made startlingly clear by a raid that the Germans launched on 6th April elsewhere on the divisional front.

See Map 4

See Map 4. The Germans fired a box barrage (that is a rain of shells that effectively cut off from all reinforcement (or retreat) a selected section of front) for one and a half hours, between 9 and 10.30 pm, on Mary Redan, a small salient jutting out from the British line, and on the extreme right of the divisional front. Divisonal boundaries were always vulnerable to such raids, especially when a division had come into a new sector; communications could easily be disrupted, and it was never quite clear which division might be under attack. The estimated eight thousand shells that were fired were sufficient to rattle the windows of the divisional headquarters at Acheux, almost ten miles away. When the barrage lifted, a German raiding party rushed the trenches (occupied by the South Wales Borderers) and made prisoner fourteen survivors, for minimum loss to themselves. This was a specialist raiding group, known as the 'Boche Travelling Circus'. The battalion suffered in total some one hundred and twenty casualties. The Germans had established that the 29th Division had taken over the sector; and they had given everyone in the Division a hard lesson in the realties of warfare on the Western Front. Almost needless to say the British retaliatory raid was a flop.

The First Battalion, Lancashire Fusiliers was commanded by Temporary Lieutenant Colonel Meredith Magniac. He was a Regular soldier, born in June 1880, who had been commissioned into the Lancashire Fusiliers in 1899. At the outbreak of the war he was a staff officer, but had been granted permission to return to his beloved regiment in 1915. He was a demanding man, and

The Sunken Road now (August 1993) and then (early hours of 1 July 1916, crowded with men of 1 Battalion, Lancashire Fusiliers).

one who led by example. On the 3rd June 1916 he was gazetted a DSO. He survived the slaughter on the Somme, but was to be killed by a shell in a communication trench not far from Monchy le Preux near Arras in April 1917. He is buried at Beaurains Road Cemetery.

Besides working on restoring the effectiveness of the trenches, the Lancashire Fusiliers also had to find some method of dominating the sunken road that lay almost mid way between the opposing trenches. It was vital that the Germans be not allowed to have the upper hand here, especially as it would make a far more satisfactory start point for the attack on July 1st, going a long way to straightening the British line, as well as obviously shortening the distance to be covered in the attack. Sunken roads were a common feature of northern France, providing ready made shelter for troops, and useful gun lines. The chief drawback was that the positions were more vulnerable to howitzer or mortar fire because they would be clearly and accurately marked on maps. This only partially damaged the feeling of comfort that these roads provided for those seeking shelter from hostile fire. The Sunken Road at Beaumont Hamel (also known as Hunter's Lane) is probably the most famous of these roads, and certainly its image is the most famous, even if viewers are unaware of what they are seeing when extracts of Malins' film on the Somme is shown.

The road was too vulnerable to be occupied with any degree of comfort — or indeed safety — during day or night, so both sides contented themselves with patrol activities in and around it. On the night of the 16th May an officers' patrol [the chief purpose of which was invariably for reconnaissance], which probably included Magniac, went out into the Sunken Road under the cover of Vickers machine gun fire which hosed the German lines with their fire. One of the officers, 2/Lt Uren, was killed and lies buried in the small British plot within the communal cemetery at Maricourt, a village at this time well behind the German lines. The Germans informed the British of his death by means of a noticeboard on their parapet. On the 18th May a smaller British patrol was threatened with being overwhelmed by a German patrol, but managed to push them off, and were left in possesion of the road for the night. By this stage it had become clear that the dispositions of the two sides would enable the British to hold the road during the day, but if both sides were to make for it under cover of darkness then the Germans would get there first.

George Ashurst was an NCO in 1/Lancashire Fusiliers, and has written an account of his Great War service in *My Bit*. He describes how he went out as one of two NCOs in a small patrol, whose task was to occupy the Sunken Road at night, and remain there until the following night. They captured the Sunken Road from the German patrol that was already in occupation easily enough. "A whisper from our officer in charge passed silently from one to another. It was the order to hurl our bombs (grenades) into the road and charge the instant he fired his revolver. A few moments later his revolver spat out; instantly our bombs whizzed through the air and at the same time we sprang forward for the sunken road. Our bombs had hardly exploded as we jumped down in the road, but Fritz had been wide awake and skedaddled back to his own lines." The patrol was immune to the German reaction of spraying No Man's Land as they took shelter against the east bank, and dug themselves small manholes in case of enemy shelling. They spent the next day in some discomfort — obviously there was no chance of making a fire, as it would give their position away: as far as the Germans were concerned, the sunken road was in its normal state of unoccupation. As soon as it was dark the Germans came out once more, in a small patrol, to occupy the road. "Breathlessly we waited for them and the crack of our officer's pistol which again was the signal to hurtle our bombs, which we gripped in our hands, the safety pins already drawn. Fritz was almost at the road when the pistol cracked. We hurled our bombs as fast as we could draw the pins and pumped bullets into them as fast as the triggers of the pistols could be pulled. Fritz certainly got the shock of his life, and with howls of rage and pain quickly made back for his own lines. Groans and shouts told us that our bombs had played havoc with them, but sharply from our officer in charge came the order, 'Back for your lives ,boys!' [The German line was rather closer to the Sunken Road — as soon as their men were back the Germans would open up with everything that was readily available: hence the need for great urgency on the part of the British patrol.] Quickly we scrambled out of the sunken road and ran as fast as possible in the darkness for our front line. Falling into shell-holes, we jumped up and ran on, not feeling the knocks and bruises in that mad dash for the safety of our front line. Fritz was beginning to light up No Man's Land now with his star lights and we knew that at any moment he would rake our wire with machine guns. Reaching our barbed wire, we dashed through the zigzag opening, tearing our clothes and also our flesh on the barbs, then jumped into the trench to lie exhausted awhile as Fritz played tunes on our wire with his bullets. That little stunt was hailed as a success, only two of our party being wounded and all of them getting back to our lines."

The number of patrols put out by the Lancashire Fusiliers was considerable, and in the tactical situation that faced them, this high level of patrolling, 'dominating No Man's Land', would seem to have justification.

86th Brigade, commanded by Brigadier General W Williams, and of which 1/Lancashire Fusiliers was a part, had obtained the services of a Tunnelling Company to construct a tunnel that would go most of the way to connecting the the British line to the sunken road. This tunnel is the one mentioned in the chapter on Malins. It was dug from Sap 7 to some seventy yards or so short of the sunken road; the divisional pioneer battalion, the 1/2nd Monmouths were to dig a communication trench to connect the tunnel at its eastern end to the road. The tunnel was opened up at 10.30 pm on June 30th, and the Monmouths had completed their task by 2.30 am.

Earlier on the 30th June the Battalion was addressed by Major General Beauvoir de Lisle, the 29th Divisional commander. A similar speech to another battalion in the Division was memorably captured by Malins film. It is, I think, of some interest to record what he actually said. "I cannot allow the Battalion of which I am so proud to enter this great battle without coming to wish you good luck, and to give you the general situation.

View from the German position known as the *Burnwurk*, looking across No Man's Land and the Sunken Road.

The Sunken Road is in the foreground, Beaumont Hamel Church visible through the shrubbery on the left; the communication trench hurriedly made on the night of 30 June/1 July was on extreme left of photograph. The Hawthorn Crater is on the far right.

We are now taking part in the greatest battle in which British troops have ever fought. At this great time all previous engagements during this and former wars sink into insignificance. The forces that are engaged in this Fourth Army are five times as large as the whole of the original Expeditionary Force.

We came out in August 1914 with four divisions, and here we have twenty one divisions. All that military thought and science can do to make this a great success has been done, for the first time we have got into position as many guns as we can and with unlimited ammunition. Now, the importance of this battle cannot be exaggerated. On the eastern theatre the Russians have had a great success. They have already captured two hundred thousand of the enemy as prisoners.

Our allies in the west have destroyed thousands of the enemy, and now we hear that the Italians are moving forward. Now, this is the chance for British troops to show that they, too, can succeed.

As you go into this great battle I want you to remember what you are fighting for. You are not only fighting to add to the glories won by past generations of the Lancashire Fusiliers. You are not only fighting to maintain the honour of the 29th Division, which won its laurels on the Gallipoli Peninsula. You are fighting for your country. More than that, you are fighting for humanity. We are fighting for truth, honour and justice. We are fighting against slavery for liberty, and we are going on fighting until we have gained our object.

39

I would like to tell you that if we are successful during the next week, we hope to gain that object before the winter. Much depends upon success, and our higher commanders know — and I know — that all their arrangments cannot win victory. Victory must be won by the infantry, and only by the infantry.

Officers and men — of all the battalions I have in this Division, you give me the greatest confidence of any. To you has been set the most difficult task — that of breaking the hardest part of the enemy's shell, and I expect you to break that shell in the German first system of trenches.

Officers and men, I wish you the best of luck, and believe with the highest confidence that what any man could do you will do, for your country."

Malins says he thought that the speech was stirring and had a great impact on the men, the faces of whom 'shone with a new light' at the great man's words. Ashurst was rather less impressed. "...as his horse pranced about our commander began to speak, raising his voice so that all could hear." His reaction? "I wonder if while he was talking he heard the ugly murmurings in the ranks or noticed our officers turning around and in an undertone order silence and issue threats. Had he heard the remarks of our men when they were dismissed off parade, he would have thought that they were not so enthusiastic about the big push."

Certainly the words do not seem inspiring; but the atmosphere and sense of tension and occasion may well have made up for that. The men's reactions were probably not so negative as Ashurst suggests — rather they were, in all probability, the standard infantry gripe of history and not particularly directed against the Big Push as such. Rather more unlikely is that the general's words, 'thrilled the hearts of every one who heard them', as Malins suggests their Divisional commander's pre-battle talk did to the London Scottish.

The Battalion actually came into the line on the evening of 30th June, and was therefore saved from a long period of tense expectancy in the trenches. B and D Companies, along with bombers, machine gunners and stokes mortars moved into the Sunken Road by 3 am. The Germans would have lost any inclination to patrol into the road because of the combination of the incessant barrage and the occasional discharge of gas over the preceding days. Once the tunnel and the final stretch of communication trench was opened up, it became possible to connect up telephone wires and have a relatively secure route for the runners to communicate with the rear. A Company was to occupy the front

Lancashire Fusiliers in King Street before the attack.

line, whilst C Company and Bn HQ were situated in Lanwick Street.

By 7 am the Germans had become fully aware of the new communication trench, and consequently would have been even more on the alert for an attack; they also spotted the body of troops now sheltering in the Sunken Road, and put a significant number of shells into the area, causing some casualties. The Lancashire Fusiliers went into action with twenty two officers and 675 Other Ranks, leaving the 'ten percent' behind to act as a rebuilding base for the battalion if the casualties were very heavy. Although the 'ten percent' is an accurate reflection of the Other Ranks who were not included in the attack, the proportion of officers that remained was much higher — more like a third. To a rather lesser extent this higher proportion applied to the NCOs as well.

As mentioned earlier in this account, the Lancashire Fusiliers held a part of the line from which it was particularly awkward to launch a coherent attack, due both to its shape and to the extent by which it was overlooked by the German positions. It would entail a careful — and complex — set of orders to ensure that the troops arrived on the German front line as a body.

When a unit or a formation was sent overseas it was required

Panorama from north-east lip of the Hawthorn Crater with the clearest possible view of the British advance across No Man's Land, between the Sunken Road and the *Burnwurk*.

to keep a record of its daily activities, in the shape of a War Diary, and return these monthly to Brigade which forwarded them to Division and so forth. The quality of the War Diary as a source of information varies widely; some included detailed orders, maps and reports on actions, whilst others are short and cursory. There is a wide variation within a battalion's diary, as the author (often the Adjutant) would change from time to time, and they had variable literary skill. In the case of a big offensive the diary did not always reflect the enormity of the action, as often the people who saw the most had become casualties. In the case of 1/Lancashire Fusiliers on July 1st the War Diary gives a coherent story of what befell the Battalion.

0720

The mine under Hawthorn Redoubt was fired, and though it was not visible from the road, all felt the ground shake. B and D Companies were now lining up in position for the assault. D Company had to be careful not to expose themselves as northern end of the Sunken Road is shallow; and B Company had to carefully select their exits as the bank is overhung and lined with trees at the southern end. 86th Stokes Gun battery opened hurricane bombardment on German first line.

0730

The leading sections of B and D and Bombing company dashed forward in extended order, being led by 2/Lts, Craig, Gorfunkle and Kershaw. At the same moment 1 platoon B Company under

Lt Whittam and 2 platoons bombers left our trenches south of Beaumont Road. A Company began to leave front line trenches in support of B and D Companies.

The leading two lines of B and D Companies had a few moments' grace, and then the enemy machine guns opened and a storm of bullets met the attack. The third and fourth lines of B and D Companies were practically wiped out within a few yards of the Sunken Road and only some wounded, including Captains Nunneley and Wells, the two company comanders, managed to crawl back.

This does not make it clear what was actually happening — or rather was meant to happen. The Stokes Mortar guns in the Sunken Road were supposed to fire as many bombs as possible on the German front line from their position in the Sunken Road. The German front line was at its closest just forward of the small wood which may be seen to-day, some two hundred yards from the Sunken Road. The men from the road would advance under the cover of this barrage of fire, would halt for a couple of minutes to reorganise, and then dash the last yards into the German trenches, where previously selected men would hold the entrances to any dugouts they might come across.

Very few men were to get close to the German wire. The battalion was a victim of the early blowing of the Hawthorn mine, and the repulsing of the attack on the Hawthorn Ridge. Standing on the northern lip of the crater, one has a tremendous view over the whole of the Fusiliers' attack, and can see how difficult was the task that faced the British. How exposed the soldiers near the Beaumont road must have felt, with little or no cover available except for the overgrown fields — and this illusory protection was being blasted away by shell fire in any case. The soldiers piling out of the Sunken Road towards the German line also had to face the difficulty of getting down the remblai, a steep embankment on the west side of the British cemetery, right under the guns of the Germans. The attack rapidly fizzled out.

A Company suffered very heavily as it made its way forward from the British Front Line, and only a few made it to the northern end of the Sunken Road; Captain EG Matthey, the Company Commander went forward with a few of his men, but was soon hit and mortally wounded. He now lies in Redan Ridge Cemetery No. 2. C Company tried to make its way forward from Lanwick Street, and was severely hit when it, too, emerged from the Front Line. One platoon was blocked by wounded in the new communication trench leading to the Sunken Road, but a group led by 2/Lt W. Caseby and sixty men reached the Sunken Road, 'though they were so encumbered with coils of wire and tools that many of them rolled down its steep banks and half an hour's delay resulted before the remnants of A and C companies could be reorganised for a further advance.'

George Ashurst was with a group of Bombers in the vicinity of Lanwick Street when the attack started at 7.30. "We set our teeth; we seemed to say to ourselves all in a moment, 'To hell with life', and as the shout of our comrades in the front line leaping over the top reached us above the din of battle, we bent low in the trench and moved forward. Fritz's shells were screaming down on us fast now; huge black shrapnel shells seemed to burst on top of us. Shouts of pain and calls for help could be heard on all sides; as we stepped forward we stepped over mortally wounded men who tried to grab our legs as we passed them, or we squeezed to one side of the trench while wounded men struggled by us anxious to get gaping wounds dressed and reach the safety of the dugouts in the rear. Men uttered terrible curses even as they lay dying from terrible wounds, and others sat at the bottom of the trench shaking and shouting, not wounded but unable to bear the noise, the smell and the horrible sights."

He crossed the Front Line trench that had been practically flattened, and dodged and weaved his way to the Sunken Road. "Miraculously, I breathlessly reached the Sunken Road, practically leaping the last yard or two, and almost diving into its shelter. Picking myself up, and looking around, my God, what a sight! The whole of the road was strewn with dead and dying men. Some were talking deliriously, others calling for help and asking for water." Ashurst offered what help he could to the wounded, which included 'one of my boys'. Then he was called to man the German side of the road by Colonel Magniac, who was preparing the men for the 8.15 attack. "...I heard the colonel calling out for all fit men to line the bank of the road, waving his revolver menacingly as he did so. Then he called for a signaller. One stepped up to him. 'Get to the top of that road and signal for reinforcements quickly,' he thundered. Without a moment's hesitation the signaller obeyed, but as he raised his flags to send the first letter the brave fellow dropped back into the road, riddled with bullets. The picture of that gallant hero's brave act will never leave my memory."

Battalion Headquarters had moved into the Sunken Road at 7 am, and so at least it was easy for Magniac to command his forward troops. He decided to try and capture the northern end of Beaumont Hamel, where the high ground offered a good field of fire, and proposed to use Caseby and a collection of seventy five men with the assistance of rapid fire from the Stokes Mortars to achieve this. However the attackers were soon caught by German fire, and only a dozen or so made it near the wire. Caseby was to survive this attack, only to die by his Colonel at Arras, in April 1917. He is commemorated on the Arras Memorial.

As Ashurst went over the top as part of the 8.15 attack he once more found himself in the midst of a fusillade of bullets; and soon afterwards decided that discretion was the better part of valour. "In a few moments I must have been alone and quickly decided to drop into a shell-hole. I felt certain that most of the men must have been killed or wounded. Anyhow, I was quite safe from Fritz's bullets, at least in my shell-hole, and I could look back over No Man's Land towards our own trenches. Hundreds of dead lay about, and wounded men were trying to crawl back to safety; their heart rending cries for help could be heard above the noise of rifle fire and bursting shells." Ashurst toyed with the idea of staying put until darkness before making a dash back for safety, but seeing some of the Royal Fusiliers on the other side of the road rushing back for the trenches, he decided that the Germans must be counter-attacking, and did not want to be caught in any British artillery barrage that might be launched. He ran back to the Sunken Road, "flinging myself into it as Fritz's bullets whistled all about me, and almost jumping on two of our men who were busy making a firing step in the side of the road." He reported to an officer, who was delighted to see him, and who put him in charge of some men at the bottom end (ie near the Beaumont Road).

There now followed a calm period in which rations were eaten, firing steps made and other measures to make the road defensible, "and we collected our dead comrades, took off their identity discs, and placed the bodies together tidily."

Another attack was planned for 12.30 pm, but this was cancelled when it became clear that Magniac had only about one hundred and twenty five effectives in the Front Line and the Sunken Road, with only a couple of officers; in addition there were over a hundred wounded men taking shelter in the relative safety of the road's banks. The battalion was ordered to make good the defences of the road (which was done under very trying conditions), and that night everyone except twenty five men and an officer was evacuated from it.

George Ashurst was one of those left in the Sunken Road overnight, being in charge of the bottom end of the road, the officer at the top, and a senior soldier with a party of seven men in the middle. The Engineers, under continual harassing fire, erected barbed wire defences for the front of the road, suffering casualties all the time.

"When daylight came the battlefield was almost quiet, friend and foe seeming to rest after the terrible strain of the day before. I and my half-dozen men were dozing, our rifles resting against the barricade, when suddenly I thought I heard voices talking on the other side of the barricade — or was I dreaming? But, snatching my rifle and jumping up, I looked over the barricade and there, standing about one hundred yards away, were three Germans, quite obviously unaware that we were still holding the sunken road." Ashurst shot one of them before the Germans dived for cover in a ditch along which they had crawled (perhaps the one to the north of the Beaumont Road that can be seen to-day?); and the garrison of the road then prepared for the inevitable German retribution in the shape of an artillery strafe. This attack caused havoc to the group holding the centre of the road. "..we heard the shouts of pain and for help and we dashed madly towards the poor fellows, regardless now of all danger. The huge shell had made a fair hit. Three of the party were killed outright and the other four all wounded. Quickly we bandaged their wounds and carried them to what we thought was the safest spot. No sooner had we moved them than another shell dropped almost in the same spot as before, hurling the three dead bodies over the road." With

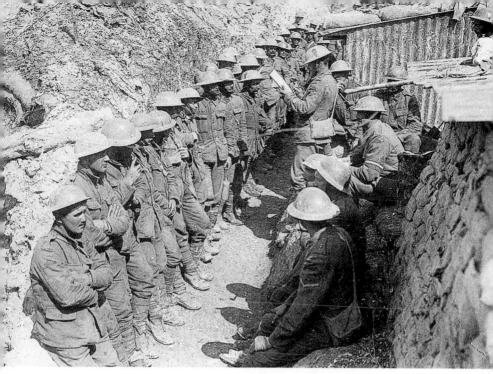

After the abortive attack on the German positions a sergeant in the Lancashire Fusiliers takes the roll — mid morning 1 July, 1916.

darkness they were ordered to evacuate the road.

The Lancashire Fusiliers, with their 'ten percent' returned to them, held the sector until July 3rd, and then moved to billets in Auchonvillers — no peace here, they were shelled by 5.9 inch guns — before the whole battalion marched to Acheux Wood, 'a very depressed force'. The battalion had lost seven officers killed and fourteen wounded; 156 other ranks killed, 298 wounded and eleven missing. The Sunken Road was incorporated into a new British Front Line, called Hunter's Lane. It was to figure prominently once more in the attack of the 51st Highland Division on November 13th, 1916.

A final note on the battles of July 1st in this area is provided in the 51st Divisional History, describing the aftermath of their successful attack in November. 'During this tour of duty an immense amount of salvage work was carried out. The whole battlefield was cleared of arms and equipment; old dumps were moved forward so as to be available for use in the consolidation of the Green Line. Large parties were also employed in collecting the dead, and loading the bodies on to waggons, so that they might be buried in the

British cemeteries at Mailly-Maillet or Auchonvillers. Parties were also employed in burying the numerous skeletons which lay scattered about the old No Man's Land. These were the remains of the troops who had taken part in the unsuccessful attack on Beaumont Hamel on July 1st. The flesh had been devoured from the bones by the rats, which swarmed in thousands, and made their homes in the empty trunks. Six hundred and sixty nine of these skeletons were buried on the front of the 152nd Brigade alone — an unpleasant task, and one which had a considerable effect on the highly-tried nerves of some of the men.' The 152nd Brigade had fought over the ground that 1/Lancashire Fusiliers and its neighbours to the right had fought over on that sunny July morning, which had started so full of promise.

One of the many casualties buried at Beaumont Hamel British Cemetery. Second Lieutenant Anderson originally came from Autralia.

48

FILMING THE WAR

The area where Malins did his filming, and most of the movements from the front line may be best seen if the car is parked by the Argyll and Sutherland Highlanders' Memorial in the Sunken Road. **See Map 6** *From there it is a matter of moving around by foot.*

Possibly the most famous single picture of the Somme Battle that rests in the popular mind is that of the Hawthorn mine being exploded on the ridge of that name. It is taken from a film on the Somme — equally well known — shot by one of the army's earliest "Official War Office Kinematographers", Geoffrey Malins. He

Malins dressed for Front Line action.

recorded his experiences in the war in a book, *How I filmed the War*, that was until recently very difficult to obtain, even on the second hand market. This problem has been solved by the (1993) republication of the work by the Imperial War Museum.

The Army was slow in getting official photographers on to the ground, but by 1916 there were a small number at work, supplemented by others from the Dominion Armies. Fortunately the early years of the war are well photographed, but only because large numbers ignored the order prohibiting cameras and set about the task themselves. Unfortunately the arrival of official photographers, and the fiercer implementation of the instruction, largely killed off the work of these amateurs, who produced work of a spontaneity and interest that still tends to be ignored by many books even in this day and age.

This also would seem to be a good moment to urge the merits of the Photographic Department of the Imperial War Museum, which house many thousands of photographs, has a generally effective indexing system for reference purposes, and a well-trained and well-disposed staff that can put you on the right track. A simple appointment is all that you need, and it is possible to have copies of photographs made for you.

Geoffrey Malins was working for Gaumont Pictures at the outbreak of the war, and had been some years in the nascent film industry. He was asked by his company to go to Belgium to get some 'stuff' (ie film), and in due course he became officially recognised as a war photographer. He was determined to get some good footage of the action on the Somme, and was directed by GHQ to the 29th Division, commanded by Major General Beauvoir de Lisle. This was early on the 26th June; de Lisle suggested that he ought to be able to get good pictures of an intense bombardment of Beaumont Hamel from Jacob's Ladder. He proceeded to this spot via Fifth Avenue, Tenderloin and King Street. At the Brigade HQ dugout he showed where he intended to film, in Lanwick Street: "We proceeded by way of King Street to Lanwick Street, and several times we had to fall flat in the trench bottom to escape being hit by shells. The whizz-bangs which Fritz puts over are rather little beggars; you have no time to dodge them. They come with a 'phut' and a bang that for sheer speed knocks spots off a flash of lightning. One only thinks to duck when the beastly thing has gone off." This extract gives some idea of the rather gung-ho way in which Malins writes of his experiences; but we would be

No Man's Land from the British side of the Sunken Road. 'Jacob's Ladder' (a series of about twenty-five steps) came off the bank some 150 - 200 yards from the photographer's position. In the banking a British bunker may still be found.

wise not to judge the man because of a literary style that seems stilted and almost a caricature to us today.

Having found his spot he had to remove sandbags (needing to expose his head and shoulders over the parapet to achieve this), and then clothed the camera in sacking and, "gently raising it on to the tripod I screwed it tight. Then gradually raising my head to the viewfinder, I covered the section which was going to be strafed, and wrapping my hand in a khaki handkerchief, waited." This latter reference to a khaki handkerchief puzzled me for a while, until it dawned that he would have to turn the handle of the camera, and his hand rotating around would quite likely catch the attention of a sniper in a notoriously risky part of the trenches.

Having taken shots at intervals for some time he then prepared to view the position in Jacob's Ladder, some yards forward of his previous position; he was taken by an officer to it: "A stranger coming upon it for the first time would undoubtedly get a slight shock for, upon turning into a traverse, you come abruptly upon an open space, as if the trench had been sliced off, leaving an opening from which you could look down upon our front line trenches, not only upon them but well in front of them. I was on the bank of a small valley; leading down from this position were about twenty five steps, hence the name Jacob's Ladder. Our parapet still followed down, like the handrail of a staircase, only of course much higher." Malins' reaction? "Jove! This is the ideal place. I will definitely decide upon it."

Malins returned behind the line to film the speech by de Lisle to men of the 2/Royal Fusiliers; Malins reports the response of the men to the great man's words of encouragement, "The faces of the men shone with a new light...."

It was soon after this that Malins heard that 'The Day' had been put off by forty eight hours. He returned to the line, and filmed the shelling of the Hawthorn Redoubt, which involved him in a hair-raising crossing of the Beaumont Road; it is easy to forget just how unwieldy a camera and tripod, not to mention associated film, actually was. He then filmed some trench mortars in action, firing 'plum puddings'. This proved to be quite a terrifying business, as there were three misfires due to faulty detonators, and the demolition of a neighbouring trench mortar pit did not encourage Malins to stay any longer than he had to.

Early on the morning of July 1st Malins was asked by Lieutenant Colonel Magniac to film his men in the Sunken Road, hitherto in No Man's Land, but which had been occupied by means of tunnelling from the main positions during the night. Malins reckons that this was the worst journey that he ever made. "I have been in all sorts of places, under heavy shell-fire, but for intensity and nearness — nothing — absolutely nothing — compared with the frightful and demoralising nature of the shell-fire which I experienced during that journey." Eventually he reached the tunnel, some two feet wide and five foot high. "Men inside were passing ammunition from one to the other in an endless chain and disappearing into the bowels of the earth... By the light of an electric torch stuck in the earth I was able to see the men. They were wet with perspiration, steaming, in fact; stripped to the waist;..." Eventually they came to the exit of the tunnel, which was about thirty feet away from a roadway, overgrown with grass and pitted with shell holes. "The bank immediately in front was lined with the stumps of trees and a rough hedge, and there lined up, crouching as close to the bank as possible, were some of our men. They were the Lancashire Fusiliers, with bayonets fixed and ready to spring forward." Having got forward, Malins had to ensure that he kept his camera as close to the bank as possible: "a false step would have exposed the position to the Bosche who ... might have enfiladed the whole road from the flank."

Malins made his way to Jacob's Ladder, filming more men en route to the front line trenches as he went. He went to find his position on Jacob's Ladder severely shelled, and further shelling brought sandbags tumbling down the Ladder. He had less than twenty minutes before the mine was due to go off, and so, "hastily fixed my camera on the side of the small bank, this side of our firing trench, with my lens pointing towards the Hawthorn Redoubt." Malins got himself ready, and at 7.19 he began turning the handle at two revolutions per second, starting this little bit earlier to ensure that he got the mine from the moment that it broke from the ground. Time passed interminably, he had used well over twelve hundred feet of film: "Would it go up before I had time to reload? The thought brought beads of perspiration to my forehead. The agony was awful, indescribable. My hand began to shake." Then it blew up, Malins finding that he had to grip the tripod as all the ground shook and swayed with the force of the explosion. Malins was completely absorbed by his filming. He

The cameraman in action.

filmed, amongst others, the Engineers leaping over the parapet with wire to secure the crater, and then some time later men went over from the parapets near him (these would be the Lancashire Fusiliers). At one stage, as the battle raged, the legs of his tripod were damaged by an exploding shell, and he had to make do and mend with bits of wood and signal wire. Later in the day Malins filmed roll calls. "In one little space there were just two thin lines — all that was left of a glorious regiment (barely one hundred men). I filmed the scene as it unfolded itself. The sergeant stood there with note-book resting on the end of his rifle, repeatedly putting his pencil through names that were missing. This picture was one of the most wonderful, the most impressive that can be conceived. It ought to be painted and hung in all the picture galleries of the world, in all the schools and public buildings, and our children should be taught to regard it as the standard of man's self-sacrifice."

Malins stayed in the Beaumont-Hamel area until the following day, and then moved on to film other sectors of the Somme battlefield. After several days of filming he went back to England to get it edited for viewing. Lloyd George said, after seeing it, "Be up and doing! See that this picture, which is in itself an epic of self-sacrifice and gallantry reaches everyone. Herald the deeds of our brave men to the ends of the earth. This is your duty." A Bishop was rather less enthusiastic, with some reason, as he pointed out the shock that might be caused to a loved one who saw her relation smiling out of her on the film and who was then subsequently killed in the battle.

Malins film is a remarkable one, despite the learned doubts about the authenticity of some of the scenes. It is now readily obtainable on a video from the IWM, along with a most useful explanatory booklet of the various scenes. Perhaps the most uncanny thing about it all is the completely divorced impression that the viewer gets: the lack of sound is almost deafening.

Hawthorn Crater to-day, clearly indicated by the trees, and photographed from the approximate position that Malins was in on July 1st 1916 (compare with the photograph on page 28).

NEWFOUNDLAND'S DAY OF HEROISM
AND DISASTER

The most useful map for following the action on the day is 7.
The Newfoundland Park is prominently signposted from the Albert See Map 7
— Bapaume road onwards. There is parking space, but this can
get congested in the summer, and in any case you are advised to
have the car parked in such a way as to make it easy to get out.
The increasing number of coaches sometimes makes manoeuvring
out a tricky operation. The visitor should also be warned to ensure
that valuables are not left in the car, or are secured in the boot, and
that the car is locked. Car theft has become quite common from
here, from the Ulster Tower and from Thiepval.

Before entering the enclosure, stand close to the edge of the road,
and with your back to the park locate the villages of Mesnil,
Auchonvillers and Mailly Maillet. The fields before you would have
been full of support trenches, aid posts, and on the Mesnil Ridge,
artillery batteries. The Newfoundlanders would have spent the night
in trenches immediately on the other side of the road, with the
majority of them on your right, the position coming across the road
on your extreme right. The Essex Regiment had a similar position
on the left. When entering the Park it is probably best to go straight
to the viewing platform on the Caribou Memorial and survey the
battlefield from there, having first read this account and studied the
map.

To get an appreciation of the strength of the position, it is
recommended to drive to Frankfurt Trench British Cemetery, off
the Beaucourt Road above Beaumont Hamel. This is in the area of
the German Second Line positions, and gives an excellent panoramic
view over Newfoundland Park. It is easy to appreciate that the
Germans here would be in an outstanding position to assist their
comrades in the Front Line with their fire and with observation for
their artillery; it seems almost miraculous that this part of the front
was ever captured.

No single regiment has the number of memorials to its memory
on the battlefields of the Great War as the Royal Newfoundland
Regiment — there are five of the distinctive Caribou memorials
scattered across the battlefields of Flanders and Picardy. No other
regiment had the honour of having the prefix 'Royal' appended to
its title during the Great War, in 1918. No other regiment has an

attack so strikingly commemorated as the Newfoundland Memorial Park does for the disastrous day of July 1 1916. And this was a regiment that did not number its battalions in tens; rather it had one — all of this for just one battalion.

Newfoundland was discovered by John Cabot in 1497 (allowing for the fact that assorted Vikings and Irish saints may well have been there first) during the reign of Henry VII. It was annexed to the English Crown in 1583 — the value of its off-shore waters (and those of neighbouring Labrador) as a fishing ground had by then become well established. Newfoundlanders were proud of their title of 'England's oldest colony'. During the Great War (in 1917) it became a self-governing colony, but united with Canada in 1949.

The caribou stands defiant above the plaques commemorating Newfoundland's missing.

During the Great War Newfoundland provided three distinct contributions to the forces of the Empire. There was the infantry, in the shape of the Newfoundland Regiment.The colonial government had originally intended to provide an infantry contribution of five hundred men in this new regiment. As things turned out this tiny population was to provide well over six thousand men for a regiment which had an outstanding war record. The second contribution, whose praises are far less widely sung, was the manpower it provided for the Royal Navy. Three hundred were killed in action or had to be invalided out of the service, whilst two thousand enlisted. Finally, Newfoundland's expertise in Forestry was utilised in a Forestry Corps, which operated in Scotland from the summer of 1917 onwards. When seen in the context of Newfoundland's population (of about ¼ million), her sacrifice of manpower is remarkable; it should explain to all who visit the battlefields why Newfoundland placed so many memorials to its Regiment on the battlefields on the Western Front.

The Newfoundland regiment made its way up to the line on the evening of June 30th; they were luckier than some unfortunate battalions elsewhere on the attack front, who spent a couple of miserable and crowded days in the trenches, and in some cases had to suffer the terrible tension of being moved out and then back again when the day for the attack was postponed from June 29 to July 1. For some unfortunates amongst the Newfoundlanders the delay was to cost their lives: a draft of sixty six reinforcements arrived on the afternoon of Friday 30th June, and many took their place in the attack the next day.

The regiment set off from their billets in Louvencourt — where they had spent nearly all their time out of the line since arriving in this part of France in April — at 9 pm. Not all of the men that See Map 13 marched were Newfoundlanders, however; Private Charlie 'Ginger' Byrne of the 2/Hampshires found himself attached to this colonial force as a Number Three on a Vickers Machine Gun. He was a trained machine gunner, but was not best pleased with his assigned post, "Number Three is the bloomin' pack-horse; he carries the ammo and gets the belts ready to feed through when each beltful is exhausted."

Just under eight hundred officers and men of the Newfoundland regiment marched out. Those left behind were the inhabitants and the 'ten percent'. This was a proportion of a battalion that was left in reserve by every attacking unit, usually commanded by the second-in-command and was designed to be the basis of rebuilding a battalion should it suffer extremely heavy losses in an attack. This sensible decision was based upon experience gained in 1915 when severe losses amongst attacking battalions — most notably at Loos — had made it difficult to restore battalions to fighting efficiency quickly. These experiences had also led to the decision to insist that commanding officers should not go over in the initial attack, but should follow on once the enemy trenches had been captured; and indeed also aimed to keep Divisional Commanders out of the firing area as well. The casualties amongst senior officers in 1914 and 1915 had been considerable, and their loss at key moments had been a cause of confusion and breakdown in command. The second-in-command of the Newfoundland Regiment was Major James Forbes-Robinson, who was to gain the Victoria Cross in April 1918 when commanding the 1/Border Regiment — he ended the war with a DSO and Bar and an MC as well as the highest award for gallantry.

The battalion marched out of Louvencourt at attention. Pte Byrne noted, however, "But, as we're swinging along, chests out, I noticed something. Well, I thought to meself, that's cheerful, that is. Right bloody cheerful, that's what. Those people lining the village street, some of them were crying. Tears pouring down their faces."

Soon after the battalion got out of the village the order came to march at ease. As they came closer to the front the battalion broke up in to single file, and they kept off the road, passing in the fields between Mailly Maillet and Englebelmer, before entering a communication trench, Tipperary Avenue which led them into St John's Road support trenches and the deep dug outs that had been dug in the preceding months. It was just after 2 am — five and a half hours before the first assault was to be made, and just over six and a half hours before the Newfoundlanders were to make their attack.

The Newfoundland Regiment's task was to be in the second wave of the British assault — they were to pass through the first wave (in their case 2/South Wales Borderers and 1/Border Regiment), regroup on Station Road and then proceed to occupy the Division's final objective for the day, having captured Puisieux Trench some two miles away, the attack commencing at 10.40 am. All the intensive training of the regiment in the preceding months had been done with this end in view: training areas near Louvencourt had been specifically selected for their similarity to the ground over which they would move at Beaumont Hamel; tapes

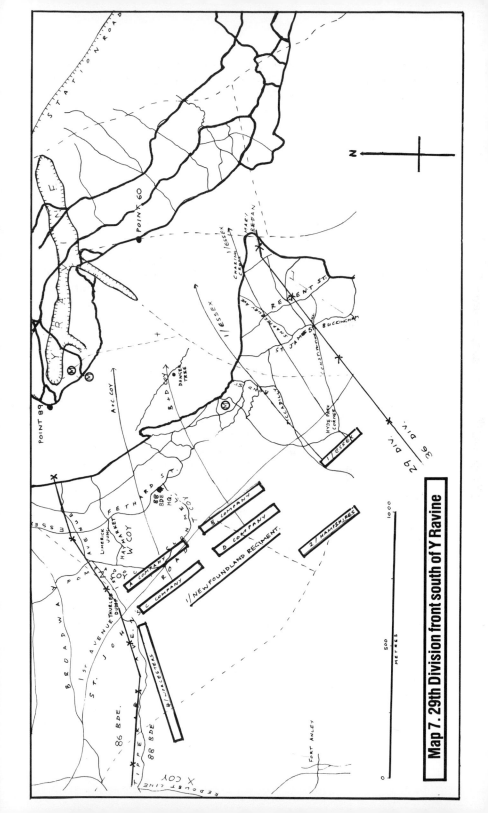

Map 7. 29th Division front south of Y Ravine

Y RAVINE

STATION ROAD

Point 60

Point 89

CHARING CROSS

1/ESSEX

1/ESSEX

MARY REDAN

MARY

REGENT ST.

ST. JAMES ST

BUCKINGHAM

PICCADILLY

ST. JAMES ST

MY. AUNT'S PASS

HYDE PARK CORNER

29 DIV.

36 DIV.

DANGER TREE

A+C COY

B+D COY

88
BDE.
HQ.

FETHARD ST.

LIMERICK JUNC.

HAYMARKET JUNC.

W COY

Y COY

1/ESSEX

B COMPANY

D COMPANY

2/HAMPSHIRES

A COMPANY

C COMPANY

1/NEWFOUNDLAND REGIMENT

RUE FETHARD

POMAVENUE

1ST AVENUE

THURLES DUMP

ST. JOHN'S ROAD

ESSEX AVE

BROADWAY

4/WORCESTERS

86 BDE.

88 BDE.

TIPPERARY AVE.

REDOUBT LINE

X COY

FORT ANLEY

METRES

1000

500

0

had been laid out to show the precise positions of German trenches; equipment that would be carried (such as ladders and portable — a misnomer — trench bridges) would fit in with the requirements for such an advance over such a well trenched area. All of this would be of absolutely no use; the Newfoundlanders would be lucky if they got even a sight of Station Road on July 1st — lucky because they would have survived the mayhem and been taken prisoner. At least they would be alive.

The men were to have the benefit of a hot breakfast — courtesy of a Corps HQ which had insisted upon this; it was carried to them from the battalion cookers by the 'ten percent' from the woods near Englebelmer. At 7.20 am they witnesed the huge explosion of the Hawthorn Mine, a kilometre or so away from their position. The attack proper commenced ten minutes later. It is important to realise that there was a pronounced German salient around the head of Y Ravine, which itself ran in an approximately west-east direction. This meant that if the defenders in the German line around Y Ravine had not been effectively dealt with by artillery fire and subsequent infantry attack, they would be in a splendid position to offer enfilade fire to the attacking troops as they proceeded in front of them; and this is what came to pass. 2/South Wales Borderers' attack folded within a few minutes; and indeed their attack made quite clear to the German machine gunners (if it was not clear before) exactly where the gaps in the British wire had been made to enable the troops to advance. All they had to do now was to concentrate their fire there and create a blockage of carnage. 1/Borderers, due to advance at 8.05 am, suffered from this fate, as well as being caught on the bridges that they had placed on the British front line to enable them to cross that particular hurdle quickly. The situation was hardly better further off to the right.

The old problem of communications now raised its ugly and lethal head. The artillery followed its strictly laid barrage plan to the minute, and thus the weight of shells continued to lift, by this time falling mercilessly on German positions to the east of Station Road. General de Lisle did order the fire of his field batteries (ie of the smaller weight guns) to be kept on the Beaucourt road — but that was at 8.40! He would have had limited influence in directing the targets of the heavier artillery, as this came under Corps Command — in any case the British only had thirty four heavy howitzers (an essential element for success) on the whole of their front. Matters were made the worse by the fact that white flares had been seen on the right of the division, which was the signal for the capture of the first objective. Unfortunately it was also a signal for the Germans that their own artillery was dropping short. De Lisle felt that he had to reinforce what seemed to be some success, and ordered two battalions of the 88th Brigade (of which the Newfoundlanders were a part) to take action to try and capture the Front Line and thus support the perceived success on the right. He issued this order at 8.37. Already the Newfoundlanders had had their advance at 8.40 halted; at 8.45 they were ordered by ther Brigade commander, Brigadier Cayley, from his advanced HQ in Fethard Street, to advance as soon as possible in support of the success on the right and to capture the enemy front line from Points 89 to 60.

It is well to realise what this means on the ground to-day. The landscape has been distorted by the growth of trees and the enclosure of the Park. There is a tendency to ignore that part of the park from the right of the entrance over to the Superintendent's Lodge. Perception is not helped by the paths that have been placed to enable the visitor and the pilgrim to make their progress around the features. The location of the cemeteries and the memorials frequently confuses people — there is an understandable inclination to think that the attack went from the general direction of the Caribou Memorial towards the 51st Highland Division Memorial,

In the distance is the superintendent's lodge. The trenches in the middle distance were the ones crossed by, amongst others, the remnants of 1 Battalion, Essex Regiment on the Newfoundlanders' right.

whereas if anything it went from the Caribou towards Y Ravine cemetery. Finally there is the problem that is raised by the names given to the various trench lines, a matter to which I shall return in due course.

The Newfoundlanders were faced with the task of an advance down a slope in an area where the enemy held a convex line — the result of which was that they would be liable to fire from various sides. Their artillery support was miles away. It was even unsure at what time 1/Essex would be launching their attack — the urgency of the moment and lack of communications made it impossible to know how they would be progressing. Perhaps it was a saving grace that all these changes had to be done so quickly, thus giving men who had expected to be on the move some minutes earlier little time to ponder on the sound of battle so close to their position, or to more than pity the wounded who must by this stage have been streaming through the support lines.

At 9.15 the Regiment set off, following the procedures laid down by the rehearsals. The CO led, then the companies; the rear two companies allowed the forward two to clear them by forty paces before following on. They all headed for the correct breaks in the wire. Before they could even begin their advance across No Man's Land they had to cross the British front trench line system and get through the front line wire. This involved moving across some two hundred and fifty yards of ground, which was under heavy shell fire and soon came under direct machine gun fire as they came over the brow of the ridge. Many Newfoundlanders were killed before they got to their own front line. The original move planned for the battalion would have taken it straight down to Station Road — in other words on the assumption that Y Ravine had been cleared of Germans. It is doubtful if there was time to retarget companies to deal with the Y Ravine position, which inevitably left the battalion vulnerable to fire from the flank.

Ginger Byrne gives a private's view of the proceedings thus far: "Things went quiet for a while. Then suddenly the bombardment started up again. It was daylight by then; lovely morning it was. I heard the rattle of machine-gun fire: you could always hear that above everything else. After a while the wounded started coming down: must have been coming up to eight o'clock by then, I suppose, but I'm not sure because I did not have a watch. The wounded was streaming down in fours and fives, one fellow helping another along; there didn't seem to be any end to them. You got to thinking that there couldn't be many left out there. Of course

No Man's Land, forward of the caribou. The approximate direction of the right of the attack would be towards the group of sheep on the left of the photograph.

you can't see anything from the bottom of a trench. So we moved out of the way for the wounded...I put the ammo boxes over my shoulder, thinking, I dunno! If we're going, I wish we'd go and get it over with. But still we stayed there.

This Officer came back, then went away. He did this about four times at about twenty minute intervals. He kept on looking at his watch. The last time he appeared he said, 'Come on lads. Time we went.'

They had a scaling ladder in this bay: that was a wooden ladder with about four rungs. The officer went first, then the other two chaps, and then me. Of course I had those ruddy ammo boxes and my rifle, so I didn't go over the top with dash as you might say — more of a humping and a scrambling really. No yelling 'Charge' or anything like that.

I kept my eye on the officer just ahead. He turned to wave us fellers on and then down he went — just as though he was bloody pole-axed. I just kept moving. I wasn't thinking really straight. My job was to keep with the gun-team. 'Don't lose me', the Number One had said. So I kept on.

And there were blokes laying everywhere."

At this stage on that July 1st morning the Newfoundland Regiment was the only unit on the move on that sector of the Front; 1/Essex had become bogged down in the dead and wounded who had filled the forward trenches and made progress for them to form up for the advance practically impossible. As for the Newfoundlanders, the original plan had been for them to walk over the top of the British lines of trenches as they made their way forward; in the light of the changed circumstances this was changed to an approach to the Front Line via the communications trenches. As for the Newfoundlanders, these trenches were hopelessly blocked with the human debris of the battle, and so they, too, had to go over the top as originally planned, but under a hail of fire. The ground over which they travelled may be viewed from near Y Ravine cemetery, looking back up the track towards the Hamel — Auchonvillers road and to the left and right of it.

The Newfoundlanders moved onwards. The 'Danger Tree' remains on the battlefield as a lone survivor of a small group of straggly trees which was some halfway across No Man's Land. It provided an ideal marking point for fire, and the shrapnel was particularly deadly in its immediate neighbourhood. Some, extraordinarily enough, did manage to make it to the German wire, but effectively it was all over for the Newfoundland Regiment by 9.45.

The CO, Colonel Hadow, from his point close to the front line, ready to follow on after his troops as orders instructed, went to inform the Brigadier that the attack had failed disastrously. He was instructed to collect what remaining sound members of the battalion that he could find and to make another attempt. Fortunately a halt was called before this particularly military form of suicide could be carried out — a staff officer from Corps who could observe the battle from Mesnil Ridge called a halt to further operations.

De Lisle now decided that the top and side of Y Ravine from Point 89 eastwards at least must be taken, and 4/Worcesters were

The Thiepval Memorial stands prominent on its ridge to centre right. The 1 Battalion Essex Regiment's attack was to run across the ground on both sides of the trees in the centre of the picture.

Y Ravine, behind the Highland Division Memorials. At this point it is some two hundred yards east of Point 89.

ordered to carry this out at 12.30, after a hurricane bombardment of half an hour. Fortunately the congested and utterly confused state of all trenches in the British front line sector made it impossible for that battalion to get to its jump-off positions and the order was cancelled. Instead, the remainder of the troops were ordered to repair the British position and prepare it for the possibility of a German counter-attack.

4/Worcesters War Diary makes interesting, if concise, reading; it was an observer to what took place, and is thus rather more coherent than some other battalions, which suffered so much in the attack.

"July 1st. Auchonvillers Sector. The Battn. was formed up as follows waiting its turn to advance. 'X' Coy, in Redoubt Line. 'Z' Coy. in Pompadour, 'T' Coy. in Clonmell, and 'W' Coy. round Haymarket. Bn. Hd. Qr. in "The Trocadero".

At 6 am a terrible bombardment was begun on the German Trenches. The Germans did not retaliate very much at this period. At 7.30 am the advance was begun by 86th and 87th Brigade. At 9 am 88th Brigade received orders to reinforce. Newfoundland Regt. went first and suffered heavy casualties from machine gun fire, Essex Regt. also pushed on, suffering casualties.

At 11.30 am the Worcestershire Regt and the Hants Regt received orders to push forward and occupy front line and prepare for a fresh attack. The Bn. suffered the following casualties in moving up, 5 Officers and 96 Other Ranks. At this time the Germans were bombarding our trenches very heavily with all kinds of shells. Telephone wires were out and communication with Brigade was kept up by runner. At about 1 pm this attack was postponed. At this period communication in the trench was very difficult, owing to the dead and wounded, the trenches, dug-outs, were badly knocked about. At 2.30 pm orders were received to hold the line at all cost, as Germans would in all probability deliver an attack. Everyone worked hard in repairing the broken trenches under most trying conditions. At 4 pm orders were received to make preparations for an attack on point 89 at 3.15 am tomorrow. Everything was ready but we had orders at 11.45 pm cancelling the advance. This order I am sure was disappointing as we were looking forward to capturing the German front line. The Battn. remained in the trenches hoping that the Germans would attack, but no luck came our way. The 10% Reserves rejoined the Battn. Germans continued to shell our trenches day and night.

July 2nd. In firing line. German artillery very active, our lines were continually shelled during the day. Commmenced to rain very heavily at 8 am. The trenches got in a very bad state, and the work of clearing the dead and wounded, repairing traverses, parapets, etc. became very difficult. Small parties went over into No Man's Land and brought in the wounded. One of our men got to a wounded man close to the German trenches, when a German officer (who must have been on the Staff by his dress) shouted to him, you must not stop there with him, if you want to come in come along or else go back to your own trenches, the lad replied "I'll go back to my own trenches, Sir". Two stretcher bearers were sent out and brought in the wounded man. At this time the Germans were acting straight, allowing our fellows to bring the wounded from No Man's Land."

The Newfoundland Regiment, after the failure of their attack, had to carry on. With the 'ten percent' and any other stragglers that had made their way back to the British position, Colonel Hadow occupied St James Street, a support trench behind Mary Redan, off to the right of the Divisional line, and outside the limits of today's park. In front of them were the remnants of 1/Essex, whilst the relatively undamaged 4/Worcesters and 2/Hampshires held the bulk of the old 88 Brigade line.

These remnants of the proud Newfoundland Regiment held this position until July 6th. In that time they were able to carry out the sad task of burying many of their comrades, often in trenches that had been abandoned, and of collecting up discarded weapons and equipment.

What became of the men of the battalion left out in No Man's Land in the blazing sun of July 1st from 10 am onwards? Many of them were wounded, and suffered terribly from thirst; others were unhurt, but found themselves unable to move, their positions being completely dominated by the Germans. Private Byrne's experience was far from being unusual.

He had managed to make it close to the German wire, when the last member of his gun crew was knocked over. "Within a yard of me there was a shell-hole — a nice new shell-hole — it wasn't big, but I couldn't see a better one handy. I was only young — nineteen. There was no one to give any orders. Boxes of ammunition aren't much good if there's no gun to fire. I couldn't see me charging the whole German army ('cos that's what it sounded like) all on my tod. I couldn't see me winning the battle by my bloody self.

It wasn't a big shell-hole, but I hadn't much choice. I slung the ammunition boxes down and I dived into it. Which was just as well: I must have been sticking out like a sore thumb by then and one of them Jerry machine-gunners decides I'm one too many still standing. Me and the bullets hit the hole pretty near together but I won.

Soldiers of 29 Division coming out of the line and marching to Albert

And there I stayed all day. I lay as I fell because I daren't move. I had my legs folded under me and my bloomin' bayonet was on my left hand side. I was dying to move that bayonet out of the way so I could get my hip down lower. But that Jerry decided he hadn't anything better to do than play his gun across my shell hole. He knew I wasn't hit. I knew what he was doing. I was a machine-gunner meself, wasn't I. He'd be holding the two handles of his gun, then he'd tap, tap so it played right across the top of the hole; then he'd turn the wheel at the bottom to lower the barrel and then he'd tap, tap the other side to bring it back again. He was hitting the dust just above my head and he smashed the blooming boxes. Bits of ammo flew about everywhere. In a queer sort of way I was lying there almost admiring what he was doing, as though it wasn't me he was aiming at. He was a fellow machine-gunner, wasn't he? And he certainly knew his job. But he just couldn't get the trajectory low enough.''

Private Ginger Byrne

Byrne suffered from thirst; he had about four inches 'of dear old Mother Earth' above his head on the side facing the Germans. He was able, however, to see what was happening in No Man's Land . ''One man lost his head and stood up and tried to run back. He'd got a terrible wound in his leg and what with the heat and everything I expect he'd gone barmy. He'd got one leg dragging and he tried to get back. He didn't get far. He got peppered. He was dead. You could see the sun glinting on those tin triangles some of them had on the backs of their packs (these tin triangles were designed to help the contact aircraft identify what was going on on the ground during the attack, so that they could report back progress being made). I lay there and watched it all. I knew there wasn't anything at all I could do until it got dark. And it was summertime. It was a long, long day.''

As dusk closed in, the Germans started lighting up the battlefield with Very lights. Byrne timed movement between the lights. ''It came down and I calculated I'd got about four seconds to stretch my legs. Another one went up further back but I wasn't bothered about that one. I moved my legs and worked my toes to get my circulation going. 'Plop' — up goes another Very light. When that was down I undid my my belt and my shoulder straps, took my gas mask off and tied a bow in it and put it around my neck. 'Plop - another Very light — so I froze. I worked out that the Jerry firing those lights was a methodical man; worked as if he were a machine — load, fire, 'plop', sizzle.'' But Byrne was also aware that the machine-gunner knew he was still there — how to get back? He got behind a nearby corpse, then crawled along, "not hands and knees, but toes and elbows, hugging the ground. It was slow work and the next light caught me cold, right in the open, so I lay stone flat. I remember thinking, Good God, I hope that gunner feller hasn't got his sights right yet. Being a machine-gunner myself I could imagine what he was doing in the trench behind me. So as the second light went down I rolled about six paces away and the dirt flew up from the place where I'd just been. Sounds silly, but I laughed to myself. The next time the Very light goes up he'll look and he'll say, 'The bugger wasn't there at all. I wonder where he's got to?' And so it went on..."

He heard stretcher bearers out doing their job, looking for the wounded under most dangerous conditions. He made it eventually into a large shell hole; one of the occupants was barely alive. He felt that he must be close to the Newfoundland line; eventually he shouted, "It's me. It's me. Where are you? Which is the way in?" There was no response at first, and eventually he bellowed

Bringing in the wounded under shell and rifle fire. This artist's impression gives some idea of what took place in No Man's Land after the disastrous attack of 1 July, 1916.

Patrol out in No Man's Land during the attack on Beaumont Hamel 1 July, 1916. The Old Beaumont Road is indicated by the line of Poplars in the middle distance. Compare this photograph with that on Page 9, a similar view to-day.

at the top of his voice. Someone directed him to a gap in the wire, "so I finally got down to the bloody trench.

And what a bloody fine mess it was too: blown all ways with shell-fire, and dead lying everywhere." He found a corporal stretcher-bearer and they returned to his shell-hole which he had left only a few minutes earlier. The corporal instructed him: " 'Get hold of his webbing.' I didn't understand. 'Bugger his equipment!' I said. So this corporal just patiently repeated, 'You get hold of his webbing, like I told you.' Then I understood. So I dug my toes in and grabbed his webbing and then between us we dragged him out and along back into the trench." Byrne left him, and scavanged to find equipment to replace that which he had abandoned — which was everything except his gas mask. He could not find anyone from either of his units; he made his way in to Englebelmer, having scrounged a meal from an artillery battery, and still unable to find anyone to tell him where to go, retired to a barn and went to sleep; he found his company the next day.

Doubtless there was nothing particularly extraordinary about Private Byrne's day on the Somme battlefield on July 1st 1916.

The Newfoundland Regiment had suffered horrendously high losses. Every officer that went over the top became a casualty — fourteen officers were killed, as were two hundred and nineteen other ranks; twelve officers and three hundred and seventy four other ranks were wounded. The officers had been ordered to wear soldier's uniforms, but Byrne can remember one in 'Sam Browne belt and riding breeches'; anyway, this precaution was wasted when all of them carried a revolver and walking stick into the attack. Like snipers of any army, the Germans made a special target of the officer. On top of these casualties was the ninety one other ranks who were missing; only sixty eight who had been in the attacking force were unwounded when it came to the roll call. Well over the ninety percent that went into the action became casualties.

There were family disasters in plenty — some especially poignant. There are the names of two sets of brothers on the Memorial Plaque at the base of the caribou memorial. Privates George and Stanley Abbott and Sergeant Stewart and 2/Lt Roy Ferguson. One family was particularly badly hit, with four cousins perishing on that same day: 2/Lts Gerald and Wilfred Ayre and Captains Eric and Bernard Ayre. The first three named died with the Newfoundland Regiment; the last was killed with 8/Norfolks fighting on the right of the British attack, and is buried at Carnoy Military cemetery.

As with so many disasters, natural or otherwise, there is often the tale of the unexpected survivor. On July 5th a soldier of the regiment crawled in from the killing ground; he had arrived with the draft that had arrived in the last hours before the attack. Completely disoriented (after all, he had missed the extensive preparations that had taken place), he had become, understandably, fed up with his lot and decided to hope for the best and approach the wire; in this case he was lucky.

The commanding officer of the regiment had watched his regiment be destroyed. Colonel Hadow was something of a strict and unbending disciplinarian, with fixed — almost immutable — views on how a battalion should be run. He also believed in training his officers to his ways. Thus the twelve new officers from the Newfoundlanders depot in Ayr in Scotland who arrived on June 15th received a far from effusive welcome from their new commander. He made it forcibly clear that he doubted the efficiency of the newcomers. Yet Hadow had won the respect of the men:

71

in the early days there was a ditty about him, sung to the tune, doubtless, of 'I'm Gilbert the Filbert':

I'm Hadow, some lad-o,
Just off the Staff,
I command the Newfoundlanders
And they know it — not half;
I'll make them or break them,
I'll make the blighters sweat,
For I'm Hadow, some lad-o,
I'll be a general yet.

Yet it was reported from the dressing station that one of the most common queries amongst the wounded was whether the Colonel was satisfied with their efforts. Veterans have agreed that Hadow was the making of the Newfoundland regiment; with a war record such as their's it is most doubtful if there could be any higher form of praise.

Certainly his reputation for ruthlessness was justified by his policy after the battle. On July 8th the battalion was removed from the forward firing area, to tents at Mailly Maillet. He immediately ordered reorganisation, and the recently arrived (June 15th) Major Forbes-Robertson carried out this order with such vigour (training parades from 5.30 am to 7.30 pm) that even an officer complained in his diary that, 'this was a bitter pill to swallow'. What price the modern trend of counselling for post traumatic disorder? Hadow realised that he had to produce an effective fighting force, and that the men should not have the time to ponder on the events of the past week. The remnants of the battalion were reinforced by a large draft, and within weeks the battalion had been restored to fighting efficiency. The Newfoundland Regiment had a lot to live up to, being the only non-regular battalion in a division composed of Regular Army units. Its subsequent war record was outstanding.

Lieutenant Colonel Hadow commander of the Newfoundland Regiment at the head of his men.

War debris near the German Front Line in Newfoundland Park.

After the war the Newfoundland Government purchased the area over which the Newfoundland Regiment had advanced. Its boundaries do not include the trenches where the Newfoundland sat in wait through the night; for the most part they lie on the far side of the Auchonvillers — Hamel road. In 1960 some of the trenches were recreated as accurately as possible to their state during the 1916 attack; in this the authorities were assisted by Captain George Hicks, MC, who fought on the 1st July as a platoon commander. This has not stopped some of the signs being misleading. Obviously the Newfoundland First Line trench was not where it is stated — it was well to the rear, as they were in support, and there were two battalions in the space between the front line trench and themselves. This is not just a technical point — the present arrangement does no service to the many Newfoundlanders who would have become casualties as they made their way to the front line; nor does it help to explain the magnitude of the task that faced them. To call it St John's Road is misleading, as well; St John's Road was the name given to the metalled road that ran between Hamel and Auchonvillers; I have yet to find a trench map that gives a name to the old British Front Line, though it may well have been known by that name. The reconstruction of the trenches, whilst admirable in purpose, provides further problems. Because these trenches have been best restored in the vicinity of the two major memorials in the Park, it accentuates the inclination to see the Newfoundlanders' attack heading off in a direction that it did not; the attack went in an easterly direction, the evidence on the Park suggests, at best, a north-easterly attack. The arrangement also tends to underplay the importance of the trenches in the part of the park dominated by the superintendents's lodge. The visitor should also be aware that this piece of ground was extremely heavily fought over on two other occasions: in November 1916 (and the attack of early September 1916, though not fought over this exact area, was close enough to have an impact) and in the period April — August 1918, in the time of the German advance and the subsequent allied Advance to Victory. The trench just forward of the Danger Tree is a relic of the attack of November 13th 1916.

The cemeteries which are to be found within the Park are described in the section of the book devoted to that matter.

Perhaps the last words on the Newfoundland attack should be left to their Divisional commander. General de Lisle wrote to the Prime Minister of Newfoundland about the attack, "It was a magnificent display of trained and disciplined valour, and its assault only failed of success because dead men can advance no further."

A view from the British Front Line trench; the Danger Tree is to the left, the plaque indicating the tree.

THE PROVING OF HARPER'S DUDS

The place most easy of access to view the bulk of the ground over which the 51st Highland Division attacked on November 13th is in the Y Ravine area. With one's back to the Highland Division Memorial in Newfoundland Park, and standing by the old German Front Line, one can view most of the ground over which 153 Brigade attacked, although the area around the west point of Y Ravine is obscured by trees. Just to the south of Y Ravine Cemetery may be seen a shallow trench line that runs across the park in a west-north-westerly direction. This was the British front line on November 13th. Looking south from the Memorial, 7/Gordons conducted the attack from the area of Y Ravine cemetery eastwards, and 6/Black Watch from there westwards. It is worthwhile making the precipitous drop into Y Ravine, just to obtain some idea of the nature of the position. Assuming one has entered the ravine by the Highland Division Memorials, proceed down the Ravine (ie eastwards). Your progress will be halted by a fence, but there is a branch of the Ravine running south; you are in the area of Y Ravine

See Maps 7, 8,9,10

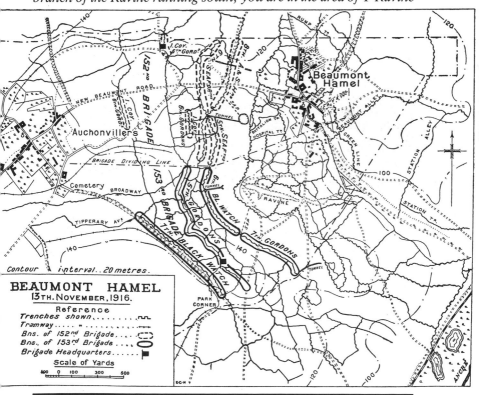

Map 8. Attack by 51st Highland Division, 13th Nov 1916

that gave most problems to the attack of the right of 6/Black Watch and the left of 7/Gordons. The numerous indentations in the side gives clear indications of man-made workings.

By following the route indicated to Hawthorn Ridge Cemetery No 1 it is possible to get excellent views north and south, and to see something of the German position that held out so stubbornly to the immediate south and east of the Crater. By proceeding along the path one can get all the way to Beaumont Hamel, veering away from Y Ravine about two thirds of the way down its length. By looking to the east one can see the strength of the German Second and Third Line positions on the high ground behind the village. In the centre of the village is the crossroads from which New Beaumont Road, Frontier Lane, Wagon, Beaucourt and Station Roads run. In the little triangle formed by the turning between Frontier Lane and New Beaumont Road, the visitor will find the base of a flag pole, a gift from the Highland Division to the people of the village. By taking New Beaumont Road, one comes to where (almost in line with the crater) one of the tanks got stuck, and another view of the strong German position in what was then a morass behind the crater (on the Beaumont Hamel side). One can return to Hawthorn Ridge Cemetery No. 1 by either taking the treacherous path up to the crater (and perhaps seeing the strange shape at its bottom, assuming it is not completely covered in undergrowth, caused by the double firing of the mine) and then following the field line towards the access road to Hawthorn Ridge Cemetery No 1; or by taking the Old Beaumont Road, until it joins the metalled road which will bring you close to that same cemetery. Of the two, the latter is likely to be the cleaner and certainly the safer, not requiring acrobatics with paths fenced off with barbed wire.

Major General Sir Montagu Harper

'It is said that General Harper first heard of the success of his Division from a wounded Black Watch private. The General was pacing up and down the road opposite his headquarters when he saw a soldier, covered with dirt, a smile on his face, and a German helmet on his rifle, limping towards him. To his inquiry how things were going he received the laconic, but pertinent, answer, "Well, anyhow, they canna' ca' us 'Harper's Duds" ony mair." '

History of the 4th Battalion, Seaforth Highlanders.

76

The Divisional sign of the 51st was an H and D interlinked — it has been incorporated into the stonework in front of the memorial by Y Ravine — and the coincidence of a commander with a surname that began with an H and the trying experience that the Division suffered at High Wood in late July and early August 1916 — resulted in this popular, if rather inaccurate, nickname. Hence the desire throughout the Division to turn the name from one with an element of truth — no matter how small — into the form of humour peculiar to the British, and with no truth in it whatsoever.

The Division had come into the Beaumont Hamel sector in the middle of October, and made preparations for the attack which was scheduled to commence on 24th October. Wire cutting operations began on the 20th October, and progress was checked each day by patrols and was recorded carefully by Divisional headquarters for the artillery and trench mortars to be redirected as necessary. The Division was to capture Beaumont Hamel and then push forward whilst the 63rd and 2nd Divisions converged on its flanks. The objectives were defined by a Green line and, further east, the Yellow line in the region of Frankfurt Trench.

The attack was also to be protected by heavy machine guns, the Vickers, firing an overhead barrage from Trench 88 in the neighbourhood of the Bowery which was aimed at the German trenches in the vicinity of the Green Line and on the western slopes behind the village. Its aim was to impair German reinforcements from coming up and to disrupt his own machine guns in their vantage point above the village. The men had to be especially briefed about this gun fire — the sound of thousands of bullets above their head might have been considered to be aimed at them, and until this time the men had not had the benefit of this type of support fire.

The attack was postponed several times because of the weather, and it was not until 10th November that the 13th November was decided upon. The ground was in an atrocious condition, with heavy downpours; little wind and clinging mists prevented the ground having any chance of drying out during the day. Mud, with the consistency of porridge, was everywhere, covering the remnants of the roads and tracks as well as everything else. At one time no more than four lorries per division were allowed on the roads, for fear that these vital arteries would be completely destroyed.

The postponements did have the advantage of plastering the German positions with even more shells, of allowing further raids

51st (HIGHLAND) DIVISION.
Circular Memorandum No. 41.

A few "DONTS" for the ATTACK.

No S.G. 2
HIGHLAND
DIVISION

(1) DONT spare time or trouble in arranging details before the
assault. No detail is too small to consider. Success lies in
thinking of and arranging for everything beforehand.

(2) DONT think you task is completed when you have reached your
objective. It is only just begun; you have got to make sure
of staying there.

(3) DONT collect souvenirs, but start work at once.
    (a) Killing or capturing every single occupant.
    (b) Making ground won proof against counter-attack.
    (c) Sending patrols or bombing parties to your front and
        flanks.

(4) DONT reinforce a trench under bombardment. The bigger the
garrison the more the casualties. Keep your reinforcements
for immediate counter-attack should the enemy attempt to
advance.

(5) DONT forget that for the protection of a captured position the
value of Machine Guns and Lewis Guns is multiplied by ten if
they are arranged to fire to the flanks and NOT to the front.

(6) DONT fail to block every Communication Trench coming into a
captured trench. If you have time always arrange to defend
it with rifle fire.

(7) DONT squander your grenades. They are difficult to replenish in
attack and you never know how badly you may want them later
on. Use your rifle and bayonet for preference every time.

(8) DONT forget to THINK because you are being shelled. Bombardments
are often very local. By moving your men a few yards to front
or flank you may bring them off scot free.

(9) DONT omit the service of protection. During a bombardment which
is the prelude to an attack a sentry must be posted over
every occupied dug-out. If the men are crouching in a trench
one man must invariably be on look-out duty.

(10) DONT think it is "all up" if you find yourself temporarily cut off
from the remainder of our troops. A Company of the West Kents
was isolated thus for 48 hours but held on and were of the
greatest value in helping on the next attack, which swept up
to and beyond the position they had held so gallantly.

(11) DONT forget the absolute necessity of frequently sending back
news to your superior. It is only by this means that
information can arrive at Headquarters and Artillery support
can be directed where required.

First
Last and
always

DONT forget you belong to the Highland Division
and
S T I C K   I T   O U T.

Ian Stewart   Lieut.Colonel,
                             General Staff,
                             51st (Highland) Division.

17th July 1916.

78

to blow up more of the wire (the Germans frequently used knife-rests here, and this form of wire entanglement was most resilient to shrapnel — it succumbed to the use of bangalore torpedoes and howitzers, however) and allowed battalions and brigades to have further extensive periods of training.

It also meant that more and better dugouts could be constructed. The Divisional history records the work done at White City: 'a chalk cliff some forty feet in height lent itself admirably to tunnelling operations. Enough head cover was provided without the necessity of making chambers to dugouts at the foot of a long flight of stairs. Full use was made of this feature, and many dugouts were hewn in it, as well as a large vault capable of holding a company, secure from the heaviest artillery.'

There were also, of course, the never-ending carrying parties. Shortly before the offensive the various forward dumps had to be filled — four hundred thousand rounds of small arms ammunition, twenty three thousand Mills grenades, sixteen hundred petrol tins of water, four and a half thousand rations, seven and a half thousand bombs, eight thousand Very light cartridges and miles of barbed wire.

The Division could also witness the morale-boosting spectacle of seeing the Schwaben and Stuff Redoubts being attacked and captured. What was particularly important was to see how effective the creeping barrage was in protecting the attackers. The more knowledgeable amongst the onlookers would also realise the importance of opening up this flank of the German Beaumont Hamel position to British observation and fire.

The attack was signalled by a mine being fired under the July 1st Hawthorn crater at 5.45 am, with the first vague signs of dawn; the artillery brought down their barrage, and the weather provided

A view from Kilometre Lane, behind the British lines.

White City Beaumont Hamel Church Hawthorn Crater

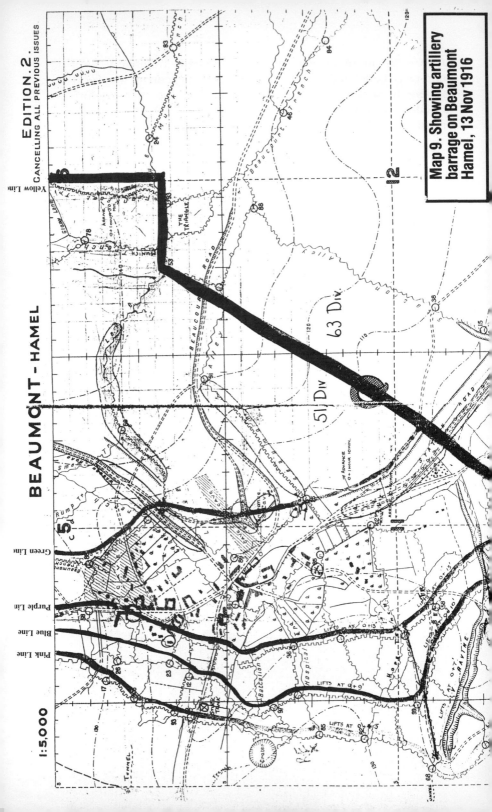

Map 9. Showing artillery barrage on Beaumont Hamel, 13 Nov 1916

BEAUMONT - HAMEL

EDITION. 2.
CANCELLING ALL PREVIOUS ISSUES

1:5,000

Yellow Line
Green Line
Purple Line
Blue Line
Pink Line

63 Div

51 Div

a thick, impenetrable fog that was to last all day. This latter was particulary important, as the German artillery signals from the front could not be seen by their artillery, and it left them blind; so long as the British infantry kept up with their barrage, they would have the vital support of shell fire.

The attack was not one of a wild charge at the German trenches; rather it was at a rate of twenty five yards a minute; when the barrage lifted off an objective the troops would rush — or rather attempt to rush — into the objective. 'The men floundered in the dark in mud over their ankles; the weight they carried was enormously augmented by the moisture that their clothing had absorbed and by the mud which glued itself to their kilts and which clung to their boots; the ground was ploughed up into a sea of shell holes half filled with water; stooks of cut strands of wire and overturned knife-rests lay everywhere. Forward movement of any kind called for considerable effort; to charge was out of the question. In some places men even became bogged up to their waists, and were unable to extricate themselves from the morass until parties of German prisoners could be organised to dig them out.'

'Let two teams dressed in battle order play football in the dark on a ploughed field in a clay soil after three weeks steady rain, and the difficulties of the attacking troops might then in some measure be appreciated.'

The attack went well, except for problems from the notorious Y Ravine, where machine gun fire from the south of it held up 6/Black Watch and 7/Gordons. They also were able to interrupt communications with those troops that had broken through on the flanks. 5/Seaforths also faced problems with uncut German wire in the vicinity of Hospital and Battalion Trench which served to break up the cohesion of the attack and lost them the protection

View across 7/Gordon Highlander's front on November 13th; the jumping off trench is to the rear of the water bowser and in front of the bank.

of the barrage; however, they were able to retrieve the situation, and infiltrated around and through the obstruction. By 7.50 am both of the attacking brigades had got through to the Purple Line, but there were many Germans still left in the ground that they had crossed, especially in pockets in the first and second line. These men had undoubtedly emerged from the great honeycomb of underground workings in the German defences.

153 Brigade, on the right, had to commit its reserves to carry Y Ravine, parts of which were being held by a large body of the enemy, possibly as much as four hundred strong. One company of 4/Gordons at each end of Y Ravine provided bombing parties which were ordered to bomb their way inwards. Meanwhile Lieutenant Colonel Booth of 6/Black Watch collected a body of men, having first established just where in Y Ravine the Germans were holding out. His task was made easier by the success of Lt. Leslie in 6/Black Watch, who had made an entrance at the western point of Y Ravine. These eventually joined up with a large group of 6/Black Watch and 5/ and 7/Gordons who had been surrounded by Germans emerging from their dugouts in the centre of Y Ravine. Between them, and with use of hundreds of Mills grenades, they were able to bomb the Ravine clear of Germans to the Purple Line.

The Green Line was then captured, and finally a body of Germans who had been able to hold out in a particularly impenetrable morass just to the east of the mine crater (at the western end of Battalion Trench) were silenced by an attack from their northern flank. The two tanks that were made available to the Division only just about made it to the German front; nothing daunted, one tank commander had his Hotchkiss machine gun taken out

A view of Y Ravine, close to its western end, looking east.

The small southward bearing arm of Y Ravine, where much of the heaviest fighting on November 13th took place.

and carried forward (by German prisoners) to be used in helping to consolidate the Green Line. The barrage had now been lost, and so the attack on the Yellow Line had to be put off — in any case, many of the troops detailed for that task had already been used to clear the extremely heavily manned German positions up to this point.

There followed a period of confusion, as attempts were made to move the attack forward; 7/Argylls did manage to capture Frankfurt Trench, but supporting troops from 2 Division lost their way, and they were forced to fall back to New Munich Trench. The battle for 51 Division was over, although it held part of the line until 17th November.

This account is particularly directed at 1/8th Argylls, their splendid memorial dominating the Sunken Road/Hunter's Trench, standing very close to the site of its battalion headquarters. There follows two accounts, the one written by the commanding officer, Lieutenant Colonel Robin Campbell, and the other by an anonymous soldier in the battalion, a member of C Company. One is a formal report, written very soon after the battle, on November 18th; the other is graphic in its description, and written some time afterwards.

Report on Operations, 13th November 1916.

On the night of the 12th/13th November, 1916, the Battalion moved up to its position in HUNTERS TRENCH. A halt of one hour was made just before the entrance to FOURTH AVENUE and hot soup issued to the men. Considerable difficulty was found in getting into HUNTERS TRENCH as it was very narrow in places, but the Battalion was ready in position at 3.20 am on November 13th.

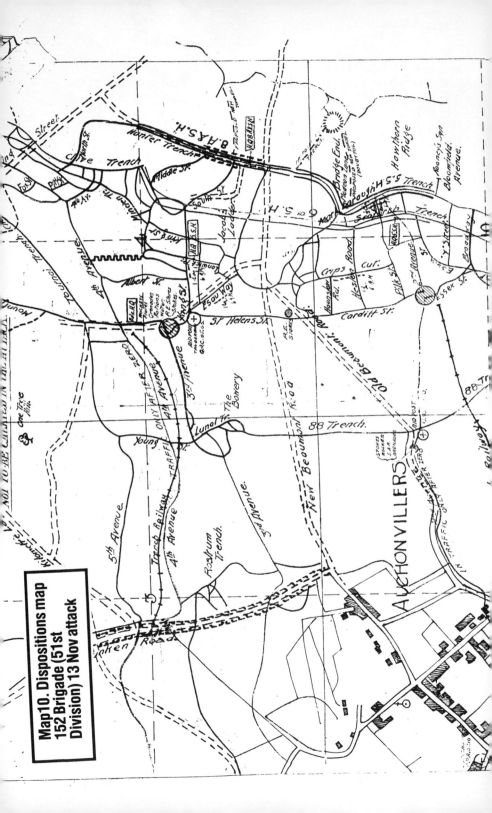

Map 10. Dispositions map 152 Brigade (51st Division) 13 Nov attack

Platoon Commanders at once set to work and cut away our wire in places where necessary. Two minutes before Zero the left of the leading wave (A Company) moved out and lay down in front of our wire in touch with 2/HLI.

Up to Zero the battalion had suffered no casualties. The mist was of great assistance in helping us get into the assembly trenches unseen.

At Zero the first wave went over followed immediately by the second, third and fourth waves. Each wave was composed of a full Company, and the Companies were placed in the order of A, B, C and D. The Lewis Guns of each company went over immediately in rear of their respective companies.

I had arranged that each wave should move out as closely as possible on the heels of the wave preceding it, as I thought that 6/Seaforths would probably be down into HUNTERS TRENCH almost before my battalion was clear of it. As it turned out the first wave of 6/Seaforths came down into HUNTERS TRENCH just as the last wave of my battalion was leaving it. The leading wave halted at about fifteen yards from our barrage [shrapnel was designed to fire forward from its burst point], and as it lifted they rushed into the front line, giving the Germans no time to get out of their dugouts. The bombing parties were busily engaged until Zero plus 20 in clearing dugouts, and they had considerable difficulty with Germans in the communication trenches.

In the meantime the second wave had carried the second line and commenced to clear it; this wave captured a minenwerfer [a German trench mortar]. They also sent down about about fifty prisoners

At 7 am Lieut. McCallum, commanding B Company, reorganised the remains of his Company and started to lead them forward to reinforce the fourth wave, but as soon as they started away from the second German line they were fired on by some Germans concealed in shell holes near the German first line. They therefore retired and dealt with this party before going on. Having done so they advanced again and eventually reinforced the leading line of the battalion.

The third wave advanced on the third German line and were entering it when the barrage lifted off it. This wave was considerably troubled by snipers on their right flank. There appears to have been a gap between the right flank of the Argylls and the left flank of the 5/Seaforth, which was afterwards dealt with by a company of the 6/Gordons. [These Germans were in the morass which held

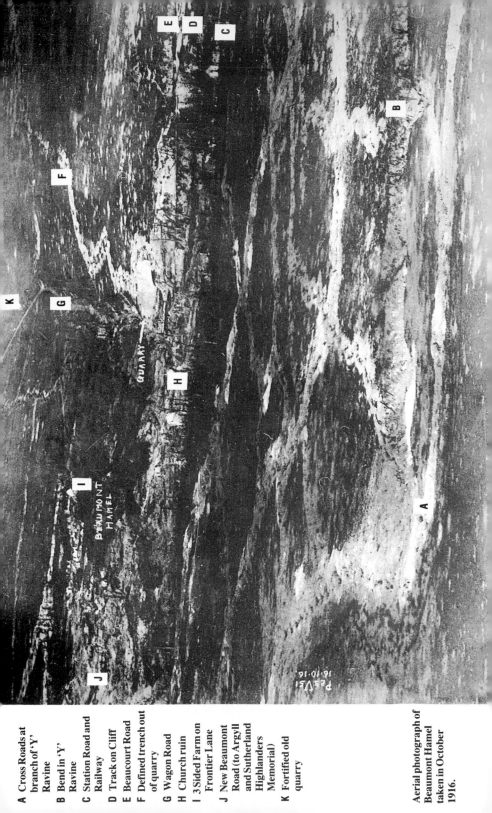

A Cross Roads at
   branch of 'Y'
   Ravine

B Bend in 'Y'
   Ravine

C Station Road and
   Railway

D Track on Cliff

E Beaucourt Road

F Defined trench out
   of quarry

G Wagon Road

H Church ruin

I 3 Sided Farm on
   Frontier Lane

J New Beaumont
   Road (to Argyll
   and Sutherland
   Highlanders
   Memorial)

K Fortified old
   quarry

Aerial photograph of
Beaumont Hamel
taken in October
1916.

out for so long to the east of the crater]. The third wave had orders to deal with two dugouts located a Q.5.c.3.5.3.5, which lay between the objectives of the second and third wave.

From information derived from a captured German map a Battalion Headquarters was suspected at Q.5.c.5.0.5.5, which was just in front of the objective of the third wave. On obtaining the objective, therefore, of the third wave, Lieut Munro, accompanied by 2/Lt Miller, went forward to search for this dugout, and there captured a Battalion commander, four other officers and a staff of forty five men (believed to be belonging to the 2nd battalion of the 62nd Regiment). [Lt W Munro was killed in May 1917 at Arras and is commemorated on the Arras Memorial.]

At 9.20 am I received information from the officer commanding the fourth wave that they had entered the fourth German line. They were afterwards shelled out of it, and retired to the third German line.

It appears a little doubtful whether this wave did actually reach the fourth German line; owing to the destructive effect of our artillery fire it was almost impossible to recognise the ground. It is, however, certain that they consolidated eventually with the third wave in the third German line, and remained there until the whole battalion moved forward later in the day to try and occupy the line of the WAGON ROAD.

The battalion was at this time (9.20 am) in touch with 2/HLI on the left and 5/Seaforths on the right.

At 4.25 pm orders were received from the Brigade to seize and consolidate the line of the WAGON ROAD from its junction with the Green Line to Q.5.b.6.3. This movement was commenced at dusk, but the advance was stopped on the Green Line from Q.5.d.1.5 to Q.5.c.8.8., and continued to hold this line until finally relieved. Contact was obtained with 2/HLI on the left and 6/Gordons on the right.

Two 'Tanks' proceeded up towards BEAUMONT HAMEL during the afternoon, but one stuck between the first and second German lines about Q.4.d.9.5 1.5; the other proceeded to the northern part of BEAUMONT HAMEL and stuck the other side of the village.

The casualties for the battalion during the fight were estimated at 250; at the present time (November 18th) they have turned out to be 265 [that is just under 40% of those who left Forceville].

The battalion front ran for some four hundred yards, from the

Auchonvillers road on the right, to the left flank which was in line with a lone blasted tree, visible near Wagon Road. The move in to the jump-off position, Hunter's Trench, was via the White City (which was to be the site of 152 Brigade Headquarters and an instant reserve of a company of 6/Gordons), King Street and Middle Street. The anonymous soldier of C Company, who was on the extreme left of the attack, takes up the story.

'Down Fourth Avenue we go, breaking step, so that the sound of our tread on the duckboards shall not travel too far, and give warning to the enemy. At intervals comes a hiss, "Mind the wire!", and we duck under a strand of telephone wire, which some benighted signaller has allowed to droop into the trench to half-strangle an unwary member of the P.B.I. [Poor Bloody Infantry]. Now a halt, then a halt, some blighter holding up the march no doubt — on again, there's White City on your left, down Middle Trench, branch off with C's rear down King Street, into Hunter's Trench, file along, or rather, fall along it — for it is carpeted with A's and B's and goodness knows how many alphabets full of leggy fighting-men — thousands of alphabets, many hitherto unheard of until one treads on a leg here, or knee there, and maybe an unwary face or two. How D will get in I don't know, but get in they will, and then perhaps the trench will burst. That's how it seems to me and many others at 3.30 am this morning of November 13th 1916. I wonder what they're doing at home now? In their little beds, no doubt, fast asleep! I could sleep too but for the fact that my opposite number squatting in the bottom of this trench has his knee planted hard against my collar bone. Can't sleep! Must get out and have a stroll! Wander into No Man's Land. Quite a number of the boys there already sitting in shell holes — more room there and more pleasant than in Hunters Trench, although a skeleton may be the occupant of the shell hole next door. I doze a little, step across to the left, and watch certain of the 2nd HLI laying a nice white tape along their front, in order that their battalion may line up on it and set off in the correct direction. I return to Hunters trench, and feeling a little chilly, get down into the bottom of it. More comfortable now, so dose off again. "Wake up — Rum ration!" I'm awake in a moment and have a wee tot. Catches one's throat a bit, but goes down and gives one a beautiful warm sensation in the "bread basket", a most luxurious feeling on a cold, misty morning, in the black hour before the dawn. Can't help feeling sleepy, but mustn't give way to sleep now. Must shake hands with a couple of my pals. I get out of the trench, find them, and wish them luck. "Same to you! See you in blighty soon!" — Alas!!

All get into Hunter's Trench now, for time is drawing on, and the mine laid in front of the 5th Seaforths on our right may at any moment give us the starting signal. I lean against the parados — feel gently melancholy — wonder if I'll see home again. Come the orders, "Fix bayonets! A Company get out and lie down!" More room now. Five minutes to go! Don't notice any signs of fear around me. Not feeling any myself (much to my astonishment), but that gentle melancholy has developed into a more familiar sensation, that sinking feeling in the pit of the stomach which comes when a meal is overdue. Three minutes to go! — beginning to get excited — two minutes — excitement mounting — one minute really excited now — half a minute! Then, unexpectedly breaking the whispering stillness, the ringing bark of a solitary eighteen pounder.

"Why's that chap firing?" "The mine's our signal!" A moment's pause — we crowd the fire steps straining our eyes towards the right, trying to see the mine go up. Hoo-oo-oom! Up she goes! The fight's on! A quarter to six has come!

A Company are off, to the accompaniment of the dull thuds of the falling clods. Crack! Crack! Crack! Crack! bark the eighteen pounders opening up one by one — crack! crack! crack! until the single explosions become merged into one continuous roar, or rather hubble-bubble, as if Old Nick's cauldron were on the boil, while at the same time "Tat-tat-tat-tat a multitude of machine guns begin rattling their messages through the air — deadly messages, leaden symbols of hate, fatal to the luckless lads who receive them. To us, waiting in Hunter's Trench, those bullets sound like falling hail, while the eighteen pounder shells, just a few feet, seemingly, above our heads go wheek, wheek, wheeking through the gloom like a concatenation of shrieking witches riding their brooms to the nether regions. Tam O'Shanter's screeching hags are a sedate selection of Whispering Winnies compared with these millions of lost souls. A noise? No! The noise. Have undergone (one cannot say hear) nothing like it before. It's no mere howling of hurricane. It's solid — and we have to get out of this trench, and bump our heads against it! What a prospect! But B Company have gone and we must follow in ninety seconds time. We get up on the firestep, place our rifles on the parapet, and scramble up besides them. Stand erect, waiting for pals to get up. The morning air does feel cold on one's bare knees! Hope none of our shells are flying too low! They seem only one foot above our heads. Pals are here. I take the first step forward, and "Jock's himself again!" No sinking feeling now! No gentle melancholy, but the wild excitement of a stirring football match intensified tenfold. Away we go with the nearest approach to a rush that that shell-torn ground will permit. Official rate of progress is twenty five yards to the minute. What my rate is, I don't know, nor do I care. I'm off. The whole battalion is off at a rate that, while leading to many of our lads being killed by our own barrage, yet enables us to surprise, and deal with, many of the Huns while they are still in their dugouts. This unofficial (undue??) haste, in fact, may make a huge success of what has been considered a more or less forlorn hope. So away we go, passing through or over a few loose strands of our wire, into the outer darkness, the dreary, mysterious waste of No Man's Land. It is very misty — and the smoke of the shells, combined with the mist, makes the morning pitch dark. On either side, keeping pace with me, are black blobs, friends no doubt! Soon they disappear, and I move along advancing quickly over, into, around, that earthy "solitaire board" of shell holes. Alone in the mist am I now, in so far as actual sight of human beings is concerned, but I know that they are there, my pals, some on either side, some behind, and many in front. Maybe I am now crossing the German Front Line, I don't know, for at this left-most point of our battalion front the trench has been blown in by shell-fire, and I can't see five yards. No doubt A Company are in the midst of a stern struggle, just a few yards to my right. The Germans are putting up a determined resistance with much bayonet work, rifle firing and bombing, and many a fine life is being blown out by the fiery breath of Mars. They pass on, their duty finished; I pass on to continue mine. Overhead the screaming shells and hailing bullets are making, still, their infernal din, while ahead is a wall of flickering flames, flashing in and out with reddish flares, as if the thousand furnace-doors of hell itself are being flung open, then closed, by fiends in waiting. Reddish flares, not calculated by any means, "to cheer a lonely sodjer on his way"! Still, a cheerier idea, they are also guiding lights. With them before me, how can I fail to go forward, even in this confounded fog? On I go. Our artillery has done its wire cutting well, for very few strands of German wire have I seen, although a part of A Company have suffered through coming across a thick belt of it, forty yards long, hidden in a sunken portion of No Man's Land. Forward then! Jump a trench — count 'One' (should have counted 'Two'). B

Company are in this trench, the second German line, and are having a very rough time of it with bombs very much to the fore. Ably and courageously led by Lieut McKellar of A Company, they are wearing down the opposition with the aid of those same Mills bombs that caused such chafing on the march up. They will clear up this particular nest of hornets, but, alas, will lose their leader when the fight is at its last gasp. This will not be until a few of C Company will have jumped over the trenches and will have been shot at from some of these dugouts not far behind them. But more of C coming on will take part in this game and, infuriated by this shooting of their comrades in the back, will "attend properly" to the thirteen Germans on the losing side. There'll be some bayonet work! Being to the left of all this, I can't see it, and, in any case, am busy counting 'Two' while taking a flying leap over a trench which appears to be ten to fifteen feet deep. See no one in it, though there is a dugout doorway just below me, as I scramble to my feet again. Should have stayed in that trench, for it is C's objective, but through miscounting, go on. Fear I'm behind time, so break into a run. Run hard into that wall of smoke and flame, thinking it must be lifting from my objective. Same old noise of hailing bullets going on above, but now the wheek-wheek of those eighteen pounder shells has changed into an even more terrifying "whizz-whizz br-r-rump fiz-z-z". Fancy the bullets are falling around me. Must be only imagination, for I haven't found my (presumed) objective yet. Won't find it either, for here the German fourth line has been blown in by our high explosive shells. Fancy those ground-bursts are going on around me now, that I can see

The material debris of war: the Somme 1916.

new shell holes actually being made as I progress through that inferno of a barrage. I get through it, right to the other side, where dawn is breaking. Then discover from the downward slope of the ground, that I have come too far, and must return through the barrage. Lose my feeling of elation — get the 'wind-up' in fact — imagine every second that I shall have one of those HEs splattering through my chest. Get back as fast as shell holes will permit without, as you can guess, making acquaintance with an HE. Meet, on the other side, a platoon of D Company, advancing (Lieut Baly at their head), in perfect order. "Where are we?" he asks. I tell him. He swings half-left and goes on. I now meet a conglomeration, an assortment, of all the Highland Regiments in the British Army, the Camerons excepted. There are Argylls, Gordons, Black Watch and HLI wandering about in the middle of a fog, plus a small wood [between Frontier Lane and Wagon Road], both singly, and in twos and threes, and all asking, "Where are we?" Having an advanced, or a 'too advanced' knowledge of the lie of the land, am able to direct them to their several units. Meet one of ours. Am just about to speak, when off he rushes to the entrance of a dugout, hitherto unnoticed, at the side of a cart-track or small sunken road. Puts his hand in at the door way of the dug out. When it emerges, between his fingers is a German ear, attached to a short, fat, dark, close-cropped Boche. Jock leads Fritz (by the ear) over to me. "What shall I do with him?", he asks, gripping his rifle by the muzzle and making playful passes, or upward jabs, at the prisoner's throat with his bayonet. Fritz, with hands stretched high is crying piteously, "Kamaraden", and shaking like a jelly. Feel somewhat disgusted with him, for I see by his bayonet knot that he is an NCO. Take pity, however, and say to Jock, "Oh, take him back!" Off they go. I join in with a couple of Argylls and am trudging back also, when one of them shouts, "There the blighters are!" and charges towards a large, black, misty body of men. I see that they are coming from our own lines, so wait until they come up. Englishmen this time! A whole company of Ox and Bucks (Oxford and Buckingham Light Infantry). Captain asks, "Where are the 2nd HLI." I tell him to turn left and he'll find them. He argues the point for a few moments, then follows my directions, and fades out of the picture. Drop back at last into my objective, C Company's line, near the dugout I had passed on my way forward. Find C, all that is left of them, busy digging out firesteps on the German side of the trench. Feel very weary but, with the inspiration of a few cuss words from our platoon officer, soon begin digging a firestep for myself at the left end of the trench. Near by 'Gibby' is busy cleaning up his beloved Lewis Gun in readiness for any counter attack that may develop. Field of fire very poor, as the wood in front obstructs view. Trench very shallow at this point. Hope we don't get shelled! Mustn't go into German dugouts until they have been properly examined, so every dugout door has a sentry, except that dugout on the right. A phosphorous bomb has been flung down there, and it is on fire, is smoking and will smoke until goodness knows when.

Finish my firestep. Talk to a sentry at a dugout doorway. Hear a voice from downstairs, "Kamerad". Sentry, with rifle to shoulder shouts, "Come up you blighter!" Up the stairs comes a lone German, hands up. As he reaches the top we see that dangling in his fingers in each hand is a revolver in a wooden case, a souvenir most highly estemed. Sentry takes one, I take the other. Ask the German are any of his friends down below still. Send him down to see. Goes down, shouts, "Fran, Hans etc", then comes up again. Says they've gone out another way. Prisoner disappears — where, I forget! Probably impressed by stretcher-bearers to aid in carrying back the wounded. A poor Gordon, wounded in the leg, lies in our trench a great part of the day. Try to get stretcher for him, but cannot, until later, for they are clearing the back areas first. We do our best for him, and he bears his pain very bravely. D Company have taken their objective, but have been shelled out, and forced to take refuge in our line. A platoon of 6th Seaforths

Cheerfulness in adversity! Mud seemingly the main enemy; working parties the perennial chore.

appears from somewhere or other, going where — they don't seem to know. Trench getting crowded so they are told to find a hole for themselves in a little post just ahead. A Company, Lieut Sloan now in command, appear at the head of a communication trench. No welcome for them here, so they settle down where they are. Don't see any dead till I wander along to our right flank. Rounding a traverse, I find three enemy dead, dark chaps, a small black growth on each chin. Each face is a assuming a sallow greenish tint. Poor fellows. Hard luck on their mothers. Afraid I'm getting too soft-hearted to be a real soldier, so move on around the next traverse. Find Lieutenants Willie Munro and Ronnie Miller there. It is C Company headquarters. Not a dugout, just an open trench with a firestep, on which they are sitting. Willie has done great things this day — captured a German colonel and his staff — but now he is really worried. With message pad on knee and pencil in hand he is considering what on earth he shall put in his next report to the C.O. The report of a bursting shell would not worry him nearly so much. With him is Lance Corporal Irwin and a couple of runners waiting to take that same report. To the C.O. it can bring nothing but the good news that his battalion has done its duty in the most gallant manner — but writing a report is a dreadful job!

The day is spent in sentry duty, resting and consuming one's two-day's rations. What we'll eat tomorrow is a question that doesn't enter our minds. Down go the rations! About 4 pm a little excitement — for the first time we see a tank coming into action. It descends the hills from Auchonvillers, gets a little way beyond Hunter's Trench, and — sticks fast in the mud. Everyone is weary, and feeling absolutely exhausted. Had no sleep last night, had terrific excitement this morning, so have been tired out since 8 am or thereabouts. Begin making ourselves as comfortable as possible under the circumstances, but orders arrive that we are to advance at 9.30 pm and take Wagon Road. Our trench fills up, A and B coming into it. At 9.30 we move off in open order, pass through the little wood, and descend the slope into Wagon Road. Much to our relief, there isn't a soul in the trench. Our barrage is playing on the slope opposite, and the 'shorts' cause us much concern. It stops at last, and we settle down peacefully. Suddenly a dark mass is seen descending the slope on our right flank. "Who are they?" is the question that immediately springs into the mind. Our right sentry post challenges them once — twice — three times — hearty, ringing challenges. No reply! We open fire and cease forthwith as a Gordon officer rushes across the road and announces that they are 6th Gordons. They had advanced on our right but had overshot their objective in the darkness. Luckily none had been hit by our shots.

We settle down once more, but within a few hours are ordered to withdraw to the former fourth German line (D Company's objective) [That is, the Green Line]. Find there most wonderful dugouts, with a number of entrances, large enough to hold a battalion. They are panelled in clean, white wood, contain real beds, stoves — home comforts, even to lingerie left, perhaps, by a German officer's lady. The ration problem is solved to a large extent by some found by the stoves, and so everything is 'trays been'. This line we hold throughout the rest day of the 14th, getting just one more thrill at the sight of two companies of the 7th Argylls making a bombing attack just in front, up the slope on the farther side of Wagon Road.

That evening the 6th Gordons relieve us. We pick up our souvenirs, German revolvers, bayonets, helmets etc., and climb out of our trench into the open once more. We wend our way slowly back in single file over the ground we have fought so hard, run such risks, to win. It is a beautiful moonlight night, and very peaceful. Hardly a gun is heard. We pick our way between the shell holes, the chalky soil appearing snowy in the bright light. As one plods along there comes to one's mind, inevitably, thoughts of the gallant comrades whom, though one cannot see them lying in their shell holes, one knows that one is passing by, probably for the last time. To many a mind, perhaps, come the word of the song:

"Trumpeter, what are you sounding now? ...
I'm calling them home, 'Come home, come home,'
Tread lightly oe'r the dead in the valley
They are lying around, face down to the ground,
And can't hear me sound the rally."

As, climbing the hill to Auchonvillers, one turns one's head for a last look at the scene, a lump comes into one's throat. But, 'Close up there!' comes the order, and on one goes again, hurried at the turn into Mailly-Maillet village by a few 5.9 [inch] shells. They choose this most awkward moment to fly at an adjacent battery'.

A couple of days after the attack was over, 6/Gordons returned to hold the defences of the village for six days, in which time they made a more extensive and detailed examination of the German defences of Beaumont Hamel. Their Regimental historian claims that Beaumont Hamel had the most complete and complex of all the German defences on the Somme, Thiepval not excluded. He goes on to describe something of the dugouts, prefacing this by pointing out that although there were existing earth works, the system was almost entirely the work of German engineers.

'In some cases the stairs leading down to the dugouts had as many as thirty or forty steps; in others there were two 'storeys', one some fifteen feet underground, and another lower still. It was estimated that one of these enormous 'burrows' could hold as many as three hundred men. Comfort as well as safety had been considered. Nearly all were fitted with beds; in some, kitchens were installed, and electric light was supplied by a power station established in the village itself. Headquarters were palatial in comfort. One Company Headquarters, within 100 yards of the original front line, may serve as an example. It was roofed with iron rails, similar to those which form the permanent way of railways, placed close together. Above these were rows of tree stems, then many feet of earth; above this again a foot of concrete covered by more earth. Outside, at the entrance, a verandah with bricklaid promenade looked out on an obelisk, a carefully constructed memorial to the German dead. The lobby leading down to the interior was lined with wood, and contained a walking stick rack. Inside were five chambers — a living room, an office, accommodation for the Feldwebel or Sergeant-Major and for orderlies, and a kitchen, which had a serving window opening into the living room. The living room was floored and panelled throughout — walls and ceiling — with wood. A table, two beds, a telephone, electric light, and a stove contributed material comfort and business efficiency, while a frieze of dark green cloth, some fifteen inches deep, and a few pictures gave artistic relief to the bare walls.'

'In another, probably a Battalion Headquarters, was found the Commander's bedroom, with chest of drawers, mirror, four-posted bed, a small table and an electric switch within easy reach, enabling the distinguished soldier to perform his arduous duties without undue risk or fatigue.'

'In the village were found a bakery, an armourer's shop and great supplies of arms and ammunition of all kinds. Large quantities of stores were discovered in a canteen: tinned beef and sardines, cigars, cigarettes (including Wills's Gold Flake), matches, coffee beans — pronounced by an expert to be Turkish, soda water, lager beer, a piano, cat-o'-nine-tails and, most treasured of all by the finder, the gallant officer who then commanded B Company, a lady's white slipper.'

The Highland Division suffered some two thousand five hundred casualties, about forty five percent of that part of the division that took part in the attack. Given the nature of the objective, and the number of the German defenders, the casualties were relatively modest. The Division took over two thousand prisoners, captured great quantities of stores and munitions, and occupied that great symbol of the potency of German defences, Beaumont Hamel. "The battle of Beaumont Hamel was the foundation stone on which the reputation of the Highland Division was built." *History of the 51st (Highland) Division.*

A German artillery Aid Post, situated in the nearby village of Puisieux. All the comforts of home in this deep dug out safe from all but a direct hit on the entrance by an artillery shell, but not fully safe from British poisonous gas.

The (51st) Highland Division memorial, modelled on a Gordon Highlander, CSM Rowan, stares across the western end of Y Ravine.

SAVING THE WOUNDED

Auchonvillers Military Cemetery and the neighbouring farm and yard are in the area of the Collecting Post. Other locations are as on the maps. It is a relatively short drive through to Mailly Maillet, Forceville and Louvencourt where Main Dressing Stations (MDS) and Casualty Clearing Stations (CCS) were located. It is in the cemeteries near these where many of the dead of a battle were buried — often even those killed outright on the field of battle — so that often provides an answer to the problem that perplexes some when they find that few of a given regiment who were killed in a particular location are actually buried there.

The work of the Royal Army Medical Corps, and indeed of the stretcher bearers provided from within the resources of individual battalions is rarely examined. The British and German armies had the best record of medical care amongst the major combatants, with a ratio of three wounded to one killed, whereas the French and Italian armies survival rate was rather worse. As the war progressed, and by the outbreak of the Somme Battle, improvements had been implemented, which aimed to ensure that men could be rapidly evacuated as methodically as possible to benefit from the developments in operative and post-operative treatment. See Maps 2, 7,10

These improvements were varied; they included increasing the number of Regimental Stretcher Bearers from sixteen to thirty two. These men had traditionally come from the band (as indeed they do today) but they were supplemented with others, and were trained in the rudiments of First Aid, but whose horrendous chief task it was to manhandle wounded men across a shell-scarred landscape, through crowded and often partially destroyed trenches, the whole often in poor weather conditions with the ground a mushy, slimy and unstable mess. Relay bearer posts were established every thousand yards, and communication trenches were built which were reserved for the removal of the wounded. Regimental Aid Posts and Advanced Dressing Stations were made more effective by being given bigger and better protected dugouts or shelters. Once some form of solid service was available, hand trollies, light railways — almost anything — was put to use. The next stage to the Casualty Clearing Stations was done as much as practicable by buses, but especially favoured was broad gauge railways, and this dictated to a considerable extent the location of these CCSs.

The job of the CCS was to retain all serious cases unfit to travel

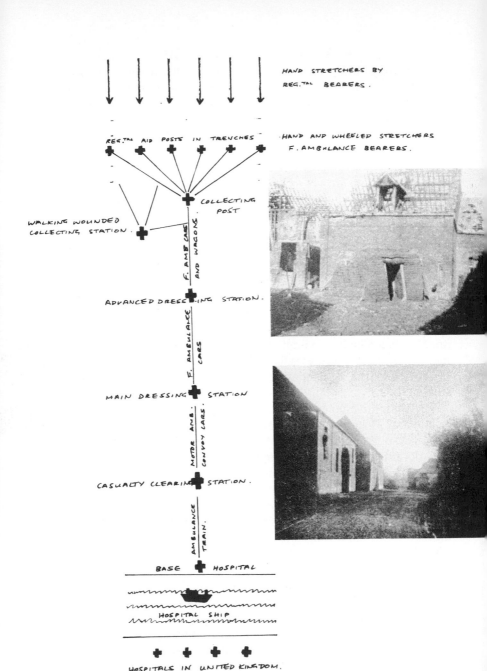

HAND STRETCHERS BY
REG.TAL BEARERS.

REG.TAL AID POSTS IN TRENCHES

HAND AND WHEELED STRETCHERS
F. AMBULANCE BEARERS.

COLLECTING POST

WALKING WOUNDED
COLLECTING STATION.

F. AMB CARS
AND WAGONS

ADVANCED DRESSING STATION.

F. AMBULANCE
CARS

MAIN DRESSING STATION

MOTOR AMB.
CONVOY CARS.

CASUALTY CLEARING STATION.

AMBULANCE
TRAIN.

BASE HOSPITAL

HOSPITAL SHIP

HOSPITALS IN UNITED KINGDOM.

Casualty collecting post at Auchonvillers. Diagram indicates the stages in evacuating wounded from the fighting.

or requiring operation before being evacuated — and this was made practicable by the presence of several consultant surgeons. They were to retain all slight cases likely to be fit for duty in a short period; and in all other cases were to evacuate the wounded to Base Hospitals further down the line. These Base Hospitals were situated well out of the fighting area, at points usually with good access to the sea for further evacuation to Blighty (hence the desire for a Blighty wound, which would ensure a considerable time, at the worst, back in Britain). The more famous Base Hospital areas were at Etaples, between Boulogne and Le Touquet, and at Rouen. Some of the biggest cemeteries are now to be found adjacent to the locations of these CCSs and Base Hospitals

Another statistic of interest lies in the cause of the wounds inflicted. The great majority of these were caused by shell or trench mortar, which accounted for 58.51%; rifle and machine gun bullets 38.98%, bombs or grenades 2.19% and bayonet 0.32%. These figures do underline the eminent WWI historian John Terraine's argument that the Great War was an artillery war.

Colonel David Rorie wrote an account of the activities of the RAMC in his fascinating book, *A Medico's Luck*, and gives a clear view of how the medical services of the 51st Highland Division operated during the November battle for Beaumont Hamel. It also enables us to view the ground over which they worked during those frantic days.

It was not only the teeth arms that learned lessons — often very expensive ones — from the fighting on the Somme as the battle went on week after week. The medical service did as well, and one of the more important innovations was the creation of the job of a Forward Evacuation Officer whose job it was to get the men out of the fighting area, that is from the Regimental Aid Posts to the Main Dressing Station and the Walking Wounded Collecting Station, a procedure that was followed right up to the end of the war.

Colonel
David Rorie

By mid October it was clear that some sort of action would in all probability be taken against Beaumont Hamel and the area around the River Ancre. When the 51st Division moved into the area it was clear that much better arrangements would be required, and the RAMC at least were pleased that the attack was subject to frequent delays. The medics faced the typical problem that improvements should be made but, "with necessarily limited RE help". This was a problem which was all too familiar to the infantry, which spent much time and labour digging fortifications and the like under RE supervision, more often than not when they were

101

supposed to be in the relatively comfortable existence of the support or transport lines.

The tasks that had to be done included the creation or improvement of Relay Bearer Posts at Tenderloin near White City, in Second Avenue Trench (this one was new) and also at Uxbridge Road, to pit prop and false-roof a Collecting Station at Auchonvillers, in an outbuilding in a farmyard and to fit stretcher racks in the cellars of a brasserie (a French pub) at Mailly Maillet, which would act as the Advanced Dressing Station. The weather at that time was particularly poor — one of the reasons for the constant postponement of the attack — and the poor Forward Evacuation Officer was exhausted not only by the dangers of the forward trenches, but by the miles of trekking through knee-deep mud.

Medical supplies were used extremely rapidly during an action, and it was essential to stockpile plenty of supplies, such as dry blankets (a nigh-on impossible task), stretchers, splints, dressings, rations and other medical stores and of course good quality water. The closer to the battle that this material could be provided the better: for example, warmth was an essential element in safeguarding men from the effects of shock. As stores were demanded from the RAPs, the Senior Officer at the Collecting Post had to make demands from the MDS, which in turn got more from the CCS. These fresh stores were generally brought up by ambulances on their return journey from carrying wounded, but because of the chronic traffic congestion that was an invariable consequence of a battle, these could be slow in coming forward: hence the need to start off with big stockpiles.

Water was always a problem, and there was always a shortage of petrol cans; despite attempts to differentiate those used for petrol from those used for water by a colour coding system, it frequently happened that the two purposes got mixed up. I can well remember talking to a veteran some time ago who was wounded at Passchendaele. He particularly remembered two things from the experience: the foul taste of petrol in the water that he was given at the RAP when he eventually found it; and the excruciating agony of the trip in the ambulance — his shattered elbow felt every jolt and judder as the vehicle went over the shell-ravaged surface. The shortage of cans was frequently made worse by the forward medical post forgetting to send the empty cans back to the next post. Another problem that faced the medics was that if the battle moved forward, the RAPs would move with it, and for this it was essential to conserve water as much as possible, as in all likelihood it would be even more difficult to obtain in the new location.

One final boost for morale was provided by placing soup kitchens as far forward to the communication trenches as possible, and voluntary groupings — in this case the Scottish Churches — provided canteens even so far forward as the Collecting Post.

The attack was launched on a foggy morning on 13th November, at 5.30 am. It is a source of some surprise to me that so much of Auchonvillers still seemed to be standing at this date — the place was barely half a mile behind the British lines, and one would have thought would have been pulverised to pulp; on this day it suffered 'hates' at 11 am and 2.45 pm, which meant that the wounded lying in the farmyard had to be brought into the cramped conditions of the Collecting Post proper.

As the afternoon progressed German prisoners were brought through Auchonvillers, and a hundred were retained at the Collecting Post to clear their own people from the battlefield. These would go off in groups, up to fifteen, under the supervision of one man. The Field Ambulance got off lightly during the battle: Captain H Begg was killed near White City, "one of the most efficient and gallant RAMC officers in the Division." He is buried at Louvencourt. Others killed included two of the German

The Aid Post near White City: possibly at Tenderloin.

PoW stretcher bearers. It was a tremendous achievement to get motorised ambulances right up to Tenderloin on the day after the attack: the ride must have been atrocious, but it was vital to ease the pressure on the severely exhausted stretcher bearers.

At daybreak on the 15th November it was possible to begin a systematic search of the battlefield to look for the wounded. An MO set off from Y Ravine twoards White City, whilst another group, accompanied by armed soldiers, in case of enemy hiding in undiscovered shelters, worked in the opposite direction towards him. "It was drizzling wet and vilely cold, the trenches in places thigh deep in clay and an awful mess of smashed barbed wire, mud, disintegrated German dead and debris of all sorts. In one trench our occupation for half an hour was hauling each other out of the tenacious and blood-stained mud; and during our mutual salvage operations we had evidently made ourselves too visible, as the enemy started shelling."

As they left a dugout after checking it, they would leave a notice indicating to the following stretcher-bearers how many wounded might be found below. They entered a complex system: "On descending about forty steps one was in a large floored and timbered chamber some fifty feet long; and at the other end a second set of steps led to a similar chamber, one side of each being lined with a double layer of bunks filled with dead and wounded Germans." These were casualties from early on the 13th November. "The place was, of course, in utter darkness; and when we flashed our lights on and the wounded saw our escort with rifles ready, there was an outbreak of 'Kamerad!' while a big bevy of rats squeaked and scuttled away from their feast on the dead bodies on the floor. The stench was indescribably abominable: for many of the casualties were gas-gangrenous. Any food or drink they possessed was used up, and our water bottles were soon emptied amongst them. After we had gone over the upper chamber and separated the living from the dead, we went to the lower one where the gas curtain was let down and fastened. Tearing it aside and going through it with a light, I got a momentary jump when caught a glimpse in the upper bunk of a man, naked to the waist, and with his right hand raised above his head. But the poor beggar was far past mischief — stark and stiff with a smashed pelvis. Some twenty other dead Germans lay about at the disposal of the rat hordes. The romance of war had worn somewhat thin here."

Colonel Rorie records one other significant memory of the Beaumont Hamel campaign. A track had been reduced to, "a

A scene from the site of Fourth Avenue and the Trench Railway that would have been used to help evacuate the wounded, looking across to Fifth Avenue (which ran by the embankment in the middle distance. At the top centre is the site of the Sucrerie (now a farm) at the end of the Sunken Road from Auchonvillers.

footpath knee deep in mud. Going up it one morning soon after daybreak, I saw a headless corpse lying on a stretcher at the path side. From the neck a trickle of blood ran to the feet of a man outside a dugout who was calmly frying some ham in his canteen lid over an improvised oil-can stove. His mate — fag in mouth — was watching him. What was beside them had ceased to be worth comment. They were surfeited with evil sights. And they were hungry."

On the 23rd November the unit was relieved, and were able to move away from the discomfort of the dugouts, usually "one long chamber with over a hundred and twenty occupants who between them produced an almost palpable atmosphere".

THE ROYAL NAVAL DIVISION'S FIRST BATTLE ON THE WESTERN FRONT

The best place to get an overall view of the Royal Naval Division attack is from the Ulster Tower on the ridge overlooking the Ancre on the south. In the season (approximately mid-May to end September) the Ulster Tower is open, and so there is the advantage of the view from the top. However, even if the Tower is closed, the line of the attack is clearly visible from the area of the entrance. From west to east may be seen Mesnil, Hamel, Beaumont Hamel snuggled away in a valley and across to the area of Beaucourt. In 1916 most of the vegetation surrounding the Ancre would have been

See Map 11

destroyed, and the banks of the river had been so shelled, and the weather so bad, that there was a great swathe of ground that was flooded or utterly boggy. The Ancre cemetery was more or less in No Man's Land on November 13th, though the British front had advanced very close The ground between the cemetery and the track running north from the road was in No Man's Land for the first few hundred yards of the track's progress northwards. The German line crossed the Hamel — Beaucourt road just to the east of its junction with the track. The site of the Redoubt, that caused so much trouble, was in the area where the track climbs notably less steeply. The ground to the west of the cemetery rises quite sharply up a ridge; it was along here that men of the Naval Division waited to follow up the attacking battalions in the front line and those who were already lying waiting for Zero in No Man's Land.

Beaucourt Station still stands, though it has recently effectively been closed. Much of the fighting took place in the siding that is to the west of the main building and platforms. Beaucourt Redoubt stood to the north of that village, at a crossroads. The church was originally closer to the Ancre; its replacement is now near the Royal Naval Division Memorial.

The Royal Naval Division was probably the most eccentric formation under British arms in the Great War. It had its origins in the realisation by the prewar Committee of Imperial Defence that there were well over twenty thousand men in the Naval Reserve

Thiepval Wood   Mesnil   Hamel Military Cemetery   Ha Chu who could not be found ships in time of war. They wanted to have a force that would be capable of seizing and holding temporary naval bases which might be needed overseas. This is how some eight thousand of these reservists found themselves training as infantry, retaining all their naval ranks and traditions, with battalion names such as Drake, Nelson, Collingwood, Hood, Hawke and so forth. These men were put in two brigades, the third brigade of the division being formed by the Royal Marine Light Infantry. To make matters even more confusing, the men retained their naval ranks and the Royal Navy cap badge. The Royal Naval Division at this stage in the war came under the Admiralty, and this explains why Winston Churchill played such a prominent part in its early history.

Winston Churchill was the First Lord of the Admiralty, a political appointment making him the head of naval matters, with Cabinet rank; the job should not be confused with that of the First Sea Lord, who was the Admiral who was the Service head of the Royal Navy. The Naval division saw action in two of Churchill's pet interventions in the war — in the failed attempt to save Antwerp, and in the fiasco that was to be the Dardanelles, or Gallipoli, campaign. Antwerp was to have a considerable impact on the fledgling force — for example the Hawke Battalion was reduced to an officer and two men, the rest being casualties, most of whom were interned in Holland.

The end of the Gallipoli campaign left the Naval Division acting as sentries on a number of Aegean Islands, whilst its fate was decided in the corridors of power in a dispute between the War Office and the Admiralty. Already the ill-will between Army and Navy that was to mar the history of the division had set in, but at least it had been decided to retain it as a fighting force and to use

Panoramic view across British and German lines north of the Ancre from close to the Ulster Tower near an old extant German machine gun position.

Newfoundland
Memorial
Park

Ancre
Cemetery

Beaumont
Hamel

the potential of its force on the Western Front rather than frittering itself away in utter tedium.

In late May the Division arrived on a number of trains at Abbeville, one of the great rail centres of the British Army, well to the rear of what was to become the Somme battlefield. The historian of the Hawke Battalion records the event: 'Never had a stranger spectacle burst upon the orthodox military eye. The battalions, the engineers, the divisional train (this refers to the supporting elements of the division), all alike had come without stores of any kind: with rifles that would only take ammunition obsolete long before the war, with all the "old soldiers" tricks and none of his experiences of the very different conditions. The material was there, no doubt, but the appearance had somehow worn off. The reports from the base camp commandant at Marseilles were hostile to a degree; the faces of the hordes of Generals and staff officers in the area of concentration were a study.'

For the next months the Naval Division was in the Souchez sector, in the shadow of Vimy Ridge. It had now been transferred from the authority of the Admiralty to that of the War Office, and had been numbered the 63rd Division, whilst retaining its distinctive subtitle of Royal Naval Division. In early October it was transferred

Officers of the Royal Naval Division soon after their arrival in France.

to the Somme, and although nothing definite in the ways of orders had been given, it was clear to all that it would be engaged in the attack on either Serre or Beaumont-Hamel.

At this early stage on the Somme, with the naval brigades in billets at Varennes and Forceville, the Division suffered the grievous blow of losing their commander, Major General Paris, who was wounded whilst on a reconnaissance. He was universally popular and respected throughout the division, had been with them from its earliest days, and perhaps most importantly was the man best able to retain the traditions of the division without antagonising its new army masters. He had an unshakeable confidence in his men and, whilst not uncritical, he had been able to keep its identity by having the confidence to promote men from within its ranks. His successor was Major General Shute, whose name could, by the simple change of a vowel, adequately sum up the opinion that most felt of him. This brought the whole business of the inefficiency, the unmilitariness and the general sloppiness that was the current opinion of the divison amongst military men to the fore; Haig in any case had an aversion to troops from Gallipoli, a prejudice discussed earlier when referring to the 29th Division.

The Divisional history is caustic about the consequences of the change in commander as the men were preparing for the forthcoming battle. 'The change in accustomed routine, in the manner of dress, in the mounting of guards, in the discipline of sentries, which followed on General Paris's departure, engaged much of the attention of subalterns and gave Colonels and Brigadiers not a moment's peace. A little later, ill-concealed rumours of a growing dissatisfaction on the part of the new Divisional Commander (which led in turn to even wilder rumours of wholesale suppressions, ending in transfer to the Army) distracted the fighting spirit of the Division still further from the matter in hand.' The Divisional history was written by Douglas Jerrold, and he also wrote the more intimate history of the Hawke Battalion; he does say that Shute became 'in later times a friend, and even an admirer, of the division'. But the early days were fraught, with the occasional moment of modest humour that could emerge from the strained relations. 'Our only triumph was when a formal complaint was lodged on one occasion by the General himself that the guard had not turned out at all. It was explained, at first gently and then firmly, that there was no guard there, but only one sentry, who as far as could be ascertained, had done everything that the drill book required for these difficult occasions.

Yet our triumph was shortlived, for General Shute, equal to any emergency, visited us in the line the next day. This time we had no answer, for it had been raining at least a fortnight, and the General's statement that the trenches were in a disgracefully muddy condition could not be denied.'

The casualties of the Battle of the Ancre were to give the army their chance to alter the character of the division, but they failed. Shute moved on to command the 32nd Division, then the 19th, then the 32nd again, and finally he was promoted and commanded V Corps. Whatever personal antipathy between Shute and the Division existed was to be resolved in later years when Shute became a Patron of the RND Officers' Association.

And so to the attack itself. The Divisional Boundary between the 63rd and the 39th was the Ancre River, such a distinguishing feature being made possible because it ran more or less in an east-west direction, and made practically necessary by the fact that the whole area around the Ancre, particularly sluggish at this stage in its course, had become a vile swamp and with the banks obliterated the river itself had considerably extended across neighbouring ground. In such circumstances difficult communications would have become impossible. This was to be the Division's first offensive on the Western Front, and most particular care had been taken with the instructions for the attack, with all ranks kept fully

Flooded section of the Ancre Valley, November 1916.

informed of what was expected of them. The method of attack was to use troops in bounds, a battalion passing through another once an objective had been captured. The first battalion would reorganise and secure the position (the failure to clear German dugouts was a cause of many of the reverses earlier in the Somme battle), and pass through the next objective in turn after its capture. The division had as its objective Beaucourt and a line just beyond it, whilst the reserve brigade was to give that extra impetus in the last stages of the battle.

Shute decided, with some justification, that the assault line needed to be straightened on the slopes above the Ancre, his aim being to ensure that attacking troops did not lose direction. This happened all too often in big attacks, a consequence of confusion, the mayhem of exploding shells, the confusion caused by trench lines when they were reached and often because of poor weather conditions; it is all the more easy to understand when one looks across the battlefield and mentally removes all vegetation, buildings and other points of reference. The concept was understandable; the problem lay in its execution, as the men from attacking battalions were the only labour available for this task. Jerrold writes in his history of the Hawke Battalion: 'The triple role of the infantry, sappers, beasts of burden, and fighting troops never pressed more heavily than it did at this place and at this time. The villages behind the line, which we of the Hawke must always associate with the rather weary period of waiting before the attack of November 13th, were Mesnil and Englebelmer. Both were entirely deserted by the civilian inhabitants, (what a surprise!) and Mesnil was only a heap of ruins covering insecurely a handful of cellars, where, when in support, we sat and shivered underground by day and night alike. Englebelmer provided at least a little comfort, though very little safety. Here by day men could walk about or sit down above ground with at least a roof over their heads. When at Englebelmer, however, we were required to supply working and digging parties to our total available strength, and a good deal beyond it every night. These parties began with a march of three miles or more to the trenches at Hamel. From there would be an impossible progress through slime and mud, either to dig assembly trenches in the open or, worse still, carrying up trench mortar ammunition. This routine was punctually carried out, but the only possible result was a high wastage from sickness directly due to over-exertion and exposure (it was late October and November when all this was going on). From this cause alone the Hawke battalion lost nearly one hundred and fifty men before the time came for it to go into action.'

One of the curious points about the 63rd Division is that one man wrote so much about it, on each occasion wearing a different hat. Douglas Jerrold wrote the Divisional history, his battalion history and his autobiography. Hence he describes the same scenario in his autobiography in a rather more bitterly personal way, in particular the carrying up of trench mortar bombs. 'The physical strain imposed on the men was far too great, largely owing to the condition of the ground and the craze for firing, from some position close to the front line, endless quantities of a peculiar kind of shell fired from trench mortars which I only remember as "toffee apples." One of these things was a strong man's load, and it took a man of quite exceptional physique to carry one from the dump up the deep slopes of the communication trenches six inches deep in sticky mud to the Trench Mortar Battery position just behind the front line.' Jerrold goes on to say that, in his opinion, and despite the weight and satsifying explosion that they produced, they seemed to be ineffectual in their task of destroying German

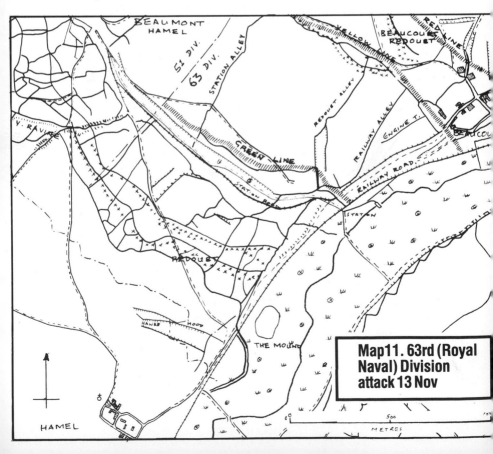

Map 11. 63rd (Royal Naval) Division attack 13 Nov

dugouts. 'It was indeed only when I ran into a party carrying these infernal machines that I ever heard the British soldier deliberately and filthily blasphemous — a well known danger signal incidentally, for ordinary"language" means nothing.'

The attack was to be launched at 5.45 am, with a creeping barrage, the main weight of heavy artillery to fall on the German front line at that time, and a barrage of field artillery to fire fifty yards short to give cover to the advancing infantry. The artillery war, so far as the British were concerned, was being fought with a new professionalism and a new confidence, so that a creeping barrage — that is artillery fire which comes down along a pre-determined line at fixed times, thereby providing the infantry with a wall of explosive protection — had a far better chance of success. The greater professionalism of the gunners meant that this had a better chance of achieving its aim, although the artillery were still bedevilled with the problem that was one of the principal causes of chaos during the war, that is poor communications. In November this was made even worse by the weather conditions.

The German line was seized, with some difficulty, but the multitude of trenches and the plethora of shell craters led to chaos amongst the attacking forces almost from the beginning. It is at times like these that a great soldier on the ground can make all the difference, and this man existed in Bernard Freyberg, whose exploits over the next days culminated in the award of a VC. His role will be discussed elsewhere.

The casualties were high, particularly amongst officers; pockets of enemy resistance continued to hold out. But the Germans were hampered by the weather as much as the British; their light signals could not be seen, and the German artillery, aware that parts of the front had been lost, were so unsighted that they were unsure where to put their own barrage. The Germans had made good use of many of the subterranean refuges that had been created during the sixteenth century French Wars of Religion; they could be turned into good dugouts where they coincided with trench systems. By afternoon the right of the attack had made progress, but things were less clear on the left, although contact was established with the neighbouring 51st Division. The following day the assault was repeated, Freyberg being assisted by elements of the Honourable Artillery Company, the HAC. Beaucourt was captured at 10.30 am; a threatened German counter attack from Baillescourt Farm, about a mile to the east of Beaucourt, was supressed by artillery fire. By the evening Freyberg had come out of the fight severely wounded, and on the morning of the 15th November the elements of the 63rd Division were withdrawn, handing over to the 37th Division.

The success of the Hood and Drake Battalions was undoubtedly considerable — and decisive; the attack on the right was particularly successful, which can in part be explained by the lie of the ground, besides the effectiveness of the men attacking. The Divisional history summarises the achievement of their attack at 7.45 am on the 14th as follows: 'the redoubt had been captured, the 188th Brigade were on the Green Line, and there was a road through to the Yellow Line to the right as well as the Yellow Line on the left of the attack. Colonel Freyberg's brilliant and gallant leadership will remain the outstanding achievement of the Battle of the Ancre but, as ever, it was the patient, the unbelievable, obstinacy, courage and endurance of the private soldier along the whole line of battle that turned the scale.' As it was, the whole division won in this battle not only a reputation, but a confidence in its own fighting capacity which contributed much to its future fighting efficiency. Such confidence is not bred of a vicarious success.'

Douglas Jerrold

Jerrold's own part in the battle was to be limited. He was the Adjutant of the Hawke Battalion, and with another officer, Leslie Wilson, he was waiting for a message to report progress, so that they could go forward and establish a Report Centre. Eventually they just set off. "I had laboriously acquired a revolver for the battle, but in my right hand I carried all the documents adjutants are supposed to carry, including even the orders for the battle, in case we ever arrived there. We knew enough by now, however, to realise that if we got anywhere at all it would be by luck, and if we got anywhere near our destination it would be by using our wits. Then suddenly, as I was trying to think if I had forgotten anything, I felt a blow and realised that my left arm had been shot off. I remembered the story of the Duke of Wellington and Lord Uxbridge. Lord Uxbridge: "They've shot off my leg, sir." The Duke: "By Gad, sir, they have." So, like the Duke, I looked round and found my arm hanging somewhere around my back, but, alas, no revolver. Indeed I walked on a few yards looking for my arm, and was really only overcome with the pleasure of finding that it was still there. Then I subsided into a shell-hole, and Wilson relieved me of such papers as he wanted, while one of our own orderlies stayed with me and bandaged my arm, with very great skill, incidentally.'

'So that was the end of my dream. No heroic exploits, no

triumphs, not even a "triumph of organisation." Just three miles of retreat in Gallipoli and thirty yards of advance in France — net gain to the enemy, 5,250 yards!'

This was the end of Jerrold's war for some time to come.

Sergeant Will Meatyard was the Signal Sergeant, 2nd Royal Marine Light Infantry (RMLI) and was with HQ Company of the battalion. The battalion was in the same brigade as the Howe, Anson and 1/RMLI, 188th Brigade. His own battalion was not going to begin their advance until fifteen minutes after the initial attack. 'About 3 am on the morning of the 13th certain platoons crawled out in No Man's Land and got close up to the German's barbed wire — there lying flat and still, patiently waiting for zero. At 5.45 am we were ready and waiting, the morning light just beginning to show itself. All watches had been synchronised. At five minutes to six the CO announced five minutes to go. What a time it seemed going. There was not a sound to be heard. The question was (and our success depended on it) was Fritz in the know — as it was nothing new for him to get wind of an attack and the time that it was coming off — but this time he was apparently taken by surprise. Each morning at dawn for the last few days our guns had been giving him pepper, and no infantry attack took place ... I expect he got fed up with these false alarms.'

Many of the casualties of the RMLI came in the muddied, shell infested No Man's Land from heavy machine gun fire and before they got to the first line. Beyond this line there was a redoubt of which the British were unaware. It was this strongpoint that had caaused so many of the casualties in the Hawke and Nelson battalions, and was to cost the latter their CO, Lt Col Norman Burge. Eventually this position was by-passed and the six hundred or so Germans that were there surrendered quite happily, given their circumstances, to a tank that was brought up against them early the folowing morning.

Sergeant Meatyard's job was to try and maintain communications as best he could, he and his signallers unravelling great coils of signal wire for the telephones. The carrying and the unravelling were the easy part of the job; the great difficulty and danger lay in repairing wire which all too frequently was broken by shell fire. When one realises that this meant finding the break, and then finding the other end which might have been blown some way away, all this in appalling conditions and hindered by enemy fire — not to mention the occasional short (ie a 'friendly' shell that fell short of its target, often on its own men) of the British, then some inkling of the perils of the task might be appreciated. '...I received orders to lay wire to a certain position ahead and with Pte Peach proceeded to lay the wire forward. We unreeled it as we went along. Almost everything had been hit by shells, and it was one continual mass of debris and mud pools. Some were half-filled with water and many had badly wounded men lying helpless in them — ghastly sights.'

With the encouragement of their CO, "Come on, Royal Marines", the 2/RMLI proceeded on their objective, Station Road. Meatyard left his recently established telephone point and prepared to move on: 'I joined on another reel of wire. Having passed a stick through the centre hole of the reel and slung my own telephone, I ran forward and the reel unwound as I went along the surface of the ground. I apparently drew the attention of machine gunners at the strongpoint (mentioned above), and also some snipers who were lurking in that direction. At about fifteen yards I dropped into a shell hole and took a breather. Then I got my legs free from the mud and made the wire ready to unreel easily. Then I made another dash and so on. As I did so each time the machine gunners opened up, but each time I dropped I think it rather deceived them as they did not know whether I was hit or not. By this means I escaped all their bullets and got to the point I was aiming at.'

Communications with the rear were in working order, and he ordered the aeroplane shutter — a means for communicating with

A remnant of Beaucourt Hamel station.

116

a plane from the ground — to be brought up ready for signalling the following morning; this so called Communicator Plane in fact only used the shutter successfully with Meatyard's battalion; otherwise it was a washout. During the morning of the 14th November Meatyard was hit. 'When I woke up I found myself in a dugout, head and arm bound up. Hadn't the slightest idea how I got there. One of the stretcher bearers of the Howe Battalion had bound me up. After a while I thought I could walk and with the assistance of one of the staff I was taken to the rear. With two other walking wounded we toddled off all together. An incident I remember was, as we passed a battery of artillery, one of the crew came up with a basin of hot cocoa and asked us to partake of it. It was a Godsend, and showed the kindness one can get at the hands of a soldier.' From here he proceeded to a Dressing Station. 'They soon got to work. I had several pieces of shell extracted from my arm, and the head wound dressed — I can't recommend the razor that was used to get the hair off!' Meatyard won a Military Medal for his part in this battle; whilst his wound turned out not only to be a 'blighty' but kept him out of France for the rest of the war.

The 1st Battalion the Honourable Artillery Company was a relatively new member of the Division, joining 190 Brigade in July 1916. 2/Lt R. Spicer was to be the first man into Beaucourt, and also had the honour to win an MC for his conduct during the battle. In his report on the battle for A Company, which he ended up commanding, he notes that the thick mist made keeping direction difficult. Snipers were a problem, but were dealt with by bombing and advancing on their positions under the cover of the weather conditions. These Germans were in the 'Hun Reserve Line', where the same old problem of dugouts which had not been mopped up provided real problems for attacking forces following on. They got through to the Green Line and commenced digging in, making contact with their neighbouring right hand battalion from a different division on the far side of the Ancre. They held their position, but came under fire from the ridge in front of Beaucourt (most likely from the redoubt of that name). Half the company took shelter under the bank of Station Road until the night came, when forward positions were once more occupied in readiness for the attack on Beaucourt and the Red Line. German machine gunners surrendered when the HAC came within some fifty yards of their position, at this stage being supported by the Hoods. The Company went straight through Beaucourt, sentries were posted at entrances to dugouts and prisoners escorted back by men from other units whilst the machine gunners opened fire on Germans now exposed in the valley in front. Eventually, at 2.30 pm on the 15th, the Company was relieved. B Company's story, from their holding position in Roberts Trench followed a similar line. Once more the bank of Station Road provided some protection against German fire; once more the company lost nearly all of its officers. The last, apart from 2/Lt A Hawes, had to be evacuated with shell shock in the early hours of the 14th to Battalion HQ. B Company too advanced through Beaucourt, with it holding the left of the battalion position, resting on the Beaucourt-Miraumont road, whilst a new strong point was being constructed near Ancre Trench. At about 2 am on the 15th the company withdrew to their original trenches in Hamel. Hawes commented: 'The stretcher bearers of the battalion did excellent work in first aid, but the stretcher and bearer parties were totally inadequate and many wounded suffered more than was necessary by being left exposed for such a long time.'

2/Lt Rowcliffe commanded D Company whose task it was to guard the extreme right flank of the attack, along the marshy parts of the Ancre. Most of the company occupied the ground from the railway line to where the ground starts its steep upwards rise; a platoon, a bombing section and the Company Lewis Gun teams, plus a couple of Lewis Gun teams from the 14th Worcesters set off from the Crow's Nest. This latter part on the extreme right lined up under cover of the Mound, and more or less lost contact with the rest of the company. This right group found the extreme left of the German position, and worked their way up it to the railway embankment, helping the advance of their own men by wiping out

The Mill at Beaucourt-sur-Ancre where the Naval Division fought in November 1916.

Soldiers attempting to clean the worst of the mud from weapons and equipment, using the waters of the Ancre in the winter of 1916.

a party of German bombers on top of the embankment. They knocked out a German machine gun firing from a dugout which was then bombed and sentries posted; all these junior officers seem particularly keen to ensure that it is made clear that they did guard these potentially very dangerous dugouts, where Germans could still be in a position to take a part in the battle. At this point men from other companies were drifting down to D Company's left, having been pushed off course by the withering fire from the redoubt. Men from D Company were then ordered to mop up the German first system of trenches, and throughout German snipers made the area around Beaucourt Station particularly unhealthy. The men had been on the go for some twenty four hours now; orders were changed at the last minute as the situation developed, under the direction, by this stage, of Freyberg. Existing orders were cancelled by 2/Lt O'Brien at 5.05 am, and the men were immediately led to assembly trenches by this latter officer. 'The men were exhausted and could scarcely keep awake.' Within fifteen minutes their objectives were outlined and the attack commenced — time was that short. As they set off towards Beaucourt the attack came under intense fire, from Beaucourt Redoubt, which kept the attackers pinned down, but the situation was salvaged by an attack that took Beaucourt from the south and an artillery barrage that provided effective cover. 'The enemy offered scarcely any resistance'.

This battle is a clear indication of how much can depend on seizing the initiative at the vital moment, on the spirit and determination of a local commander, on weather conditions (the fog served the attackers far better than the defenders) and on luck. One instance serves to illustrate this; soon after Beaucourt was captured, it was found that the British heavy artillery was shelling the north east corner of the village still, risking British lives and the consolidation of the position. Carrier pigeons were sent to inform the artillery of the new situation on the ground, all other means of communication having failed, and runners being far too slow. Almost immediately the gunners lengthened their range. Where does luck come into this? The HAC history tells us that, 'for the first time in action, as far as the Battalion was concerned, messages were successfully forwarded by carrier pigeon to Brigade HQ.'

THE HERO OF THE ANCRE: BERNARD FREYBERG VC

The viewing positions and maps are the same as recommended in the preceding chapter on the Royal Naval Divison.   See Map 11

'At nightfall on the 13th, after the most bloody casualties, it was realised that the attack had again failed, but Lieutenant Colonel Freyberg, though wounded, collected every man who had got through the left of the German defences. This party of about 350 he led during the night up the spur to attack Beaucourt Redoubt. He took the redoubt and the remainder of the ridge, and next morning 5,000 Germael Freyberg won the battle of the Ancre. Probably this was the most distinguished act of the war.'
General Sir Beauvoir de Lisle, former GOC 29 Division, writing in *'The Story of the 29th Division.'*

After the withdrawal of the Royal Naval Divison from Gallipoli, Freyberg, with many others of the Hood Battalion, was able to go to England on leave. The fate of the Division was hanging in the balance, especially as the surplus of Royal Naval Reserve no longer existed. In fact he had determined to transfer to the Army, the commander of his Brigade recommending a man who had won the DSO, had been given command of his Battalion, and had been wounded. Amongst other things he wrote, 'Commander Freyberg is gifted with the highest instincts of fearlessness, determination and leadership, and I cannot speak too highly of his admirable qualities. I am very pleased to record my high appreciation of him, with my strong recommendation for special employment in which these qualities are especially needed.' In May 1916 he was gazetted a Captain in the Royal West Surrey (The Queen's) Regiment, and made temporary Lieutenant Colonel commanding the Hood Battalion.

It was, perhaps, the arrival of Freyberg and fellow officers in London at this crucial time in the RND's history that ensured its survival, more or less, in its post Gallipoli form, albeit with the addition of an army brigade. The greatest influence has been ascribed by some to AM ('Oc') Asquith, the Prime Minister's son. There were many others who were influential in the Division, such as the Hon Vere Harmsworth, son of Lord Rothemere, proprietor of the Daily Mail. He was to be killed just beyond the redoubt that caused so much trouble early on in the November battle, and

The young Freyberg

Vere Harmsworth

is now buried at the Ancre Cemetery. Rupert Brooke had been a member, others were prominent in literary and social circles — it had a high proportion of very intelligent and articulate men in its ranks.

It was to the hugely different warfare of the Western Front that Bernard Freyberg went in late May 1916. The RND spent the summer being inducted into these unaccustomed ways, a training period that was resented by many in the Division, but accepted by more level heads as a necessary part of adaptation to European war. The Battle of the Ancre was a long time coming, suffering frequent postponements; this inevitably produced considerable strain on all those concerned, as for a period of a month the Division was kept on two day's standby for the attack.

When the great day came, the Hood Battalion was on the right of the Division and just to the left of the River Ancre. The minutes before the attack were tense, with the plan of attack requiring great numbers of troops to be packed in to a small area. Just before the start, Freyberg visited the forward units. "On the extreme right I stopped to talk to Kelly, who commanded B Company. I wanted to take both his hands and wish him 'God speed', but somehow it seemed too theatrical; instead we talked rather awkwardly, and synchronised our watches. I walked back along our sector, speaking to the men I recognised." One of those who spoke to Freyberg on that cold, dank and misty morning was Joseph Murray, who wrote in *Call to Arms*: "I fancy I can see a figure approaching on my left; maybe it's a ghost; I cannot hear any footsteps and there is no reason for anyone to be wandering about; we are all supposed to be sleeping. After what seems to be an eternity, I realise it is no ghost; it is the colonel, Colonel Freyberg, who is having a quiet chat with the chap in the next hole to me. I sit up with much difficulty. He apparently recognised an 'old hand'...'You, too, are still with us. So pleased to see you.

Beaucourt station.

The old church at Beaucourt, which was to the south and east of its present positon, in March 1916.

Make yourself as comfortable as you can and good luck. Do try to get some sleep.' With these parting words he disappears in the darkness."

The attack was launched at 5.45 am on November 13th, and the battalion set about its task. The first line was nothing more than an outpost, with resistance centred on the trenches immediately to the rear. This was honeycombed with deep dug-outs, connected to each other and to the second line, several hundred yards further back. They were lit with electricity and, in one case at least, were a hundred feet deep. The artillery had done its job, and the trenches were battered and smashed beyond a recognisable line — compasses, watches and the progress of the barrage were the only means of fixing position, as landmarks were non-existent. Lessons had been learnt — dug out entrances were lit up by the phospherous bombs that had been thrown down them, to minimise the risk of Germans coming up behind the advancing British troops.

The plan had by this stage broken down, with battalions being held up by the redoubt in the German front line to the left of the Hood attack. It was at times like these in the Great War that so much depended on the initiative of battalion commanders. Chief Petty Officer Tobin comments on the situation after the first rush: "...over the rise I saw Colonel Freyberg just prancing along all alone (his Adjutant and Signal Officer had been killed on the way up). He looked grand as he always did in battle, spick and span, in his best uniform. He said to me: 'Hello, Tobin, I think we will get a VC today."

So, by 8 am, the attack had been ground down, with the single notable success of the Hood Battalion, having moved to the Green Line. But the troops that were due to pass through them on to the Yellow Line had been largely destroyed in their advance. Freyberg decided that he would have to attack with what troops were available to him, making full use of the barrage that was timetabled to fall shortly before 9 am. They succeeded in capturing Engine and Beaucourt Trenches, but Beaucourt, tucked in behind a small ridge, remained in German hands. The Divisional commander (Shute) had decided to keep up the barrage because he was afraid, with some justification, that Freyberg's men might be cut off, due to the failure of the attack on the left. The rest of the day and night was spent in the region of the Yellow Line. Perhaps the worst aspect of this position was the constant number of British shells that 'dropped short' — nothing could be done about it, because there was little prospect of a runner getting back alive with a message. Freyberg gives us this description of being under shellfire. "We could hear the report of the 9.2-inch guns being fired, and we strained to hear the sound of the approaching shells; first we heard a whistle which quickly swelled into a roar, culminating with a tremendous concussion; the impact of the earth of the quarter-ton projectile driven at that rate through the air was frightening — quite the most vicious sound imaginable." That going on for many hours is a ready explanation for shell shock.

There were, even then, lighter moments. A large German ration and postal dump had been captured, and the joys of cigars, cigarettes and some liquor helped to calm nerves during these tense hours. "My orderly room clerk discovered a jar of liquor, rather like rum in appearance and strength. After having drunk a good deal, he climbed out of the shell hole, and lay in full view of the enemy position, his commander thought, killed. He lay there all the afternoon until dusk, when they pulled him in by the legs, to find him untouched!"

During the night reinforcements had arrived, and Freyberg extended his left. Confusion was rampant, as several different battalion were now in the line, with several different, and frequently contrary, orders. Despite all this, the attack went ahead; Freyberg was hit, "I had not gone ten yards when a bullet hit my tin helmet, breaking my chin strap and knocking me on my back." He was not hopeful of great success, when suddenly hundreds of Germans emerged from dug-outs to surrender. Freyberg had already been wounded twice, and was wounded a third time when an egg grenade found him caught up in barbed wire; although he hit the ground (so far as that was possible) he was hit by several splinters. Although the village was captured, it was essential to move the hundreds of troops that were bearing down on it out of the village before the Germans launched a fierce artillery barrage, once the fact of its loss had been confirmed. It was soon after this that Freyberg's career with the RND was to be brought to an end: "...then there was a bang, a curious ringing note in my ear and I lost consciousness. When I came to my head gave me a good deal of pain, and as I lay downwards hot blood was dropping from my nose and chin. I thought at first my head had been smashed, but I located the wound in my neck with two dirty fingers." He had suffered a huge gash, which had stripped the muscle to the vertebrae. Freyberg's main concern was to warn the other battalion commanders that he was out of action, that they would have to shift for themselves and work through General Shute.

He was able to walk back (with assistance) to the RAP, situated by Railway Road at the foot of a steep bank. It was at this point that the pressure and physical injury had their impact on the man: "With the loss of blood, and the immobility, all resistance broke down, and it was a much frightened man who was carried back along the shelled road. At the field dressing station he was at first put in a tent reserved for those who should be made comfortable before death overtook them; a Captain Greaves had him removed and treated him. In 1941, in Cairo, Freyberg asked Greaves if he had been on the Ancre in November 1916 — he had recognised him simply by his voice.

The wounded await further evacuation. Note the dockets on some of the men, indicating the nature of the wounds and treatment given.

In mid-December 1916 his award of the Victoria Cross was announced in the Gazette, the citation ending: 'The personality, valour and utter contempt of danger on the part of this single officer enabled the lodgement in the most advanced objective of the Corps to be permanently held, and on this point d'appui the line was eventually formed."

Bernard Freyberg, the small boy from Richmond, Surrey who had emigrated with his parents to New Zealand and then returned to England when grown up, had achieved one of his great ambitions. He was to go on to even greater things. He returned to the Hoods in March 1917, but just two days before an attack near Arras in late April, he was appointed a Brigade commander (173 Brigade) of the 58th (London) Division. He had just turned twenty eight years old, and was the second youngest Brigade commander in the war — only 'Boy' Bradford held such a command at a younger age. In January 1918 he was moved to command the 88th Brigade, in the 29th Division — another connection with the Ancre sector of the Somme — and including within the Brigade the Royal Newfoundland Regiment. He also earned the unusual distinction for a brigade commander of winning not one but two DSOs — the last one for an action that ended at 10.59 am on the 11th November 1918. He was to add another one to his collection in 1945, during the Italian campaign.

After the war Freyberg stayed in the army — but as a Captain in the Grenadier Guards. Promotion followed steadily, until he retired as a Major-General in 1937. Soon after the outbreak of the Second World War he was chosen by the New Zealand Government to command their forces; he was C-inC in the ill-fated Crete adventure, and after the war was Governor-General of New Zealand, from 1946 to 1952. He returned to England and was appointed Lieutenant-Governor of Windsor Castle, where he lived until his death. In 1922 he was married, in the remote and ancient church of St Martha's, near Chilworth on the hills above Guildford, sited on the old pilgrim's route to Canterbury. He died in 1963, and he lies now in that Churchyard surrounded by the

Bernard Freyberg VC

beauties of the Surrey countryside. His gravestone says simply: Freyberg VC.

THE TANK AND THE BATTLE OF THE ANCRE: NOVEMBER 1916

The two areas to examine here are those where the tank actions took place. The strongpoint mentioned in the first account is reached by parking the car by the Ancre British Cemetery and walking up the (initially) metalled road that climbs up the ridge immediately to the east of it. After some four or five hundred metres, as the track rises less steeply, and on both sides of the track, is the approximate site of the redoubt. It is not advised to bring a car up here, as the metal of the road soon gives way to a farm track, and there is nowhere suitable for a car to turn around.

See Maps 9, 11,15

The Triangle is to the north of the Beaucourt Road, just below much of which ran the trench of that name. It occupied a vaguely triangular piece of ground, meeting the road at a point where a track runs directly south, some three hundred yards east of the track leading to New Munich Cemetery. From here it ran a hundred yards or so in a northerly and north westerly direction, being connected at the top. The strength of the position may be appreciated without moving far from the road.

Functioning or not, a sight like this towering above one would unnerve most defenders.

The tank had made its first appearance on the Somme at the Battle of Flers-Courcelette on 15th September. It is no part of this account to dwell on that event, or the days that followed. The press had greeted its arrival in the most extravagant terms, a view that was not shared by the staff. To be fair to them, it had considerable defects, it was extremely slow, it was very cumbersome and it was all too vulnerable to being bogged down in the entrenched and shell-smashed ground across which these lumbering monsters had to operate. It is appropriate, however, to quote Basil Liddell Hart, a formidable proponent of the tank in the inter-war years, and no friend of General (as he then was) Sir Douglas Haig, on that man's view of the tank as expressed on 17th October 1916, when the tank had been engaged in several actions.

"Haig's own reaction was more favourable than that of most of his staff and subordinate commanders." He met the commanders of the embryo Tank Corps (formally established in July 1917) at his Advanced HQ and "thanked them warmly for what had been done and said that, although the tanks had not achieved all that had been hoped, they had saved many lives and fully justified themselves." He added, according to an observer, 'Wherever the tanks advanced we took our objectives, and where they did not advance we failed to take our objectives.' "He then said that he wanted as many tanks built as possible, while suggesting that these should have improved armour and be of a heavier type." He sent a senior officer a couple of days later to a conference at the War Office to demand a thousand new tanks, whilst a hundred of the Mark I were ordered until a new design could be finalised.

By the middle of October 1916 it became finally apparent that the advances of the Fourth Army, occupying for the most part the area of the battlefield to the south of the Ancre, was floundered in the sea of mud which was now the dominant feature of the Somme. This mud was considered by many of the combatants to be even worse than that which characterised the later Paschendaele conflict a year or so later. But the incessant nibbling away at the Pozieres Ridge, at the villages along the Albert-Bapaume road, and the gradual eating away of the ground to the north of this Somme Via Sacra of the British army, had left much of the German position north of the Ancre in a salient into the British attack. This made it more vulnerable to that most potent weapon of the Great War, the Artillery. It was determined that the Reserve Army under General Gough should launch an offensive to clear this German stronghold.

With this end in view, the remaining tanks were transferred to that Army for refitting at Acheux, and a total of fifty two tanks found themselves detrained there. As time progressed, some twenty or so were transferred back to the main front. To get a good idea of the sheer nastiness of the Somme fighting at this stage, I can recommend no better book than Sidney Rogerson's, *Twelve Days*, recently republished.

The Reserve Army (it became the Fifth at the end of October) made plans for the attack on the German held ground astride the Ancre, but had to make repeated postponements because of the weather conditions. A number of tanks spent their time being shuttled around the Somme front; inevitable, given their small numbers, but unfortunate in that it did not allow the tank commanders to develop a sound knowledge of the ground over which they would have to operate. The bad weather did not help morale, especially as the men were billeted in poor conditions; whilst the tension caused by the frequent postponements effected everybody.

At the beginning of November tanks were moved up (via Beausart) to Auchonvillers and La Signy Farm. However, once in these lying-up places, the heavens seemed to open completely. Aerial photography played a vital part in enabling commanders to make a decision about the role of the tanks in the future conflict: 'the old shell holes and many of the old trenches had filled up with water, and ... the greater part of the front was in a hopeless condition for that type of Tank (Mark I).'

On November 12 nearly all the tanks were sent back from La Signy Farm, and most of those at Auchonvillers; instead of being used as an integral part of the initial offensive, they were to be made available should the advance provide an opportunity for their use on firmer ground further ahead. The tanks that were assisting the assault south of the Ancre took their part in the main

Winter on the Ancre. Water iced over in the craters.

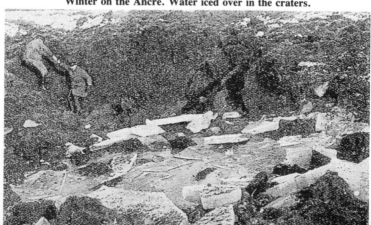

assault, and played a useful role in what was a largely successful operation.

The tanks to the north of the Ancre played a vital part in removing two enemy strongpoints, though not on the first day. Two tanks were led by a trench mortar officer, Lieutenant Alan Campbell, RNVR, to deal with the strongpoint in the German front line trench that had been the cause of so many casualties to the battalions on the left flank of the 63rd Naval Division attack. Whilst so much progress had been made adjacent to the Ancre, and Freyberg was leading his men to the capture of Beaucourt, this redoubt proved to be extremely stubborn, and threatened to be a major obstacle to the British advance.

Despite the shell-torn terrain, the tanks managed to make their way to the German front line; the first crossed the German trench, but became bogged down almost immediately afterwards. The second fared worse, becoming stuck just before the German front. However, the lead tank still had a six pounder gun that it could use, and the tank commander used the limited means of visibility available to him to see how this weapon could be best used. The sight that greeted him was extraordinary, and is here recorded as witnessed. The ground before him seemed to be shimmering with white, "on opening the front flap of the tank and obtaining a better view, it was seen that all the German garrison, some four hundred in number, appeared to have found something white to wave in token of surrender; those who could not produce anything better were waving lumps of white chalk about or bits of board or rifle stocks which they had rapidly chalked white. The situation was rather an embarrassing one for so small a number as the crew of two tanks to deal with; fortunately, however, it was possible by signs, and with the assistance of the infantry, to mop up these four hundred prisoners before they realized that both the tanks were stuck and out of action."

Forty two men of B Company, 14/Worcesters, the Divisional Pioneers, were to spend four hours on the morning of the 15th November slogging away to salvage these two bogged down monsters. This was not the only work that had to be done; the British advance had brought the infantry up against new obstacles — but also to firmer ground. The task that was faced was to make it possible for tanks to proceed over the ground that had been won. Because of the extremely heavy shelling that it had suffered over the preceding days (not to mention preceding months) the land was all but impassable. By the end of the 17th November only one tank had been able to make it through the churned morass to a position where it could be used to assist the attack; all the others had become bogged down hopelessly.

This one tank had to be made to count. It was decided that its objective should be the Triangle, a German strongpoint roughly midway between Beaumont Hamel and Beaucourt just above the Beaucourt Road. The hard frost of the last night or so had helped to make it easier for the tank to make its approach, although the ground immediately around the redoubt had been heavily shelled; the tank was to attack from the flank in support of the frontal infantry assault. To assist the tank a route was taped for some distance ahead of the British front by the Tank Intelligence Officer to show it the way; once more time was too short to enable the tank commander to make any sort of adequate reconnaissance.

However, this plan was to be thwarted by a fall of snow which covered the tape shortly before the tank was to move forward. Once more the Intelligence Officer stepped into the breech. He had been over the ground before, and determined that the only solution was to lead the tank to its position — he had strict orders not to enter a tank. He walked over the British front line, made his way through shell holes filled with freezing water and took it up close to the Triangle, coming through the operation unscathed despite the hail of bullets flying around him. He then returned to the British front whilst the tank proceeded to roll up the German line. It was impossible for the German artillery to open fire on it because the tank was in the midst of the German lines, and it was able to use its machine guns to devastating effect both in the immediate vicinity and also on the German transport lines.

The infantry attack became held up elsewhere and the tank was required to remove stubborn points of German resistance. It was

Repairing the roads — a never ending, but vital, occupation on the Somme in the autumn and winter of 1916.

impossible to make contact with the tank other than by runner, and once more the Intelligence Officer made his way across the field of battle and guided it home to the Brish lines to prepare it for a new attack. Perhaps fortunately for the exhausted crew and its pilot, the ground had thawed, and it proved to be impossible to get the machine back into action again.

Few in numbers and hampered by the terrible condition of the ground, hindered by the primitive state of battlefield communications and a victim of ghastly weather conditions, the tank had played a not inconsiderable part in the battle waged north of the Ancre and in those areas where it succeeded.

The remarkable Intelligence Officer was Captain (later to rise to the rank of Major General) FE 'Boots' Hotblack. *HQ Tanks 1917 — 1918* provides a pen portrait of some of the chief characters of the command element of the early days of the Tank Corps, and Hotblack takes his place amongst those described. Before the war he had been a brewer, and was a gifted linguist. From the time of his commissioning (in September 1914) he had played an important role in Intelligence, serving as a liason officer in the days of the retreat. He served in various HQs, and made a name for himself as being unafraid of risk, and frequently appearing at dangerous points on the front. "He was about six feet two inches tall, and always moved very swiftly and silently on india-rubber soles. He had unusually large eyes, the largest I ever saw; talked very little, and seemed almost to resent being talked to; was a fanatic about the war, thought of nothing else, and concentrated the entire energies of a very capable brain on his immediate job. He was a natural soldier. His sense of duty, his standard of dsicipline, his extreme efficiency, and his astonishing courage were an invaluable asset for the Corps (to which HQ he was transferred at the end of September 1916). No other department was better run than his, and he was never subject to the criticism that used from time to time to be directed against other members of the staff, that they were not sufficiently in touch with the actualities of the situation."

As a result of his actions at Beaumont Hamel he was to add a DSO to his MC; he was also to ensure the high regard that Intelligence Department was to hold in the Tank Corps — and indeed his portrait hung in the Officers Mess of the Intelligence Corps for many years, a fitting tribute for a pioneer 'Intelligencer'. He was invalided out of the army afer an accident in April 1940, shortly after assuming command of the 2nd Armoured Division.

A TRAGEDY OF WAR.

In recent years the controversy over capital courts martial during the Great War has grown in intensity. This was triggered by Judge Anthony Babington's somewhat circumspect book, *For the Sake of Example*, published in 1983. This was followed by the far more detailed analysis of individuals, with details including names and places of burial, by Julian Putkowski and Julian Sykes in *Shot at Dawn*. Both of these books have raised considerable questions about the proceedings that took place against these men who suffered the ultimate penalty for crimes relating only to military discipline, such as desertion and cowardice or for crimes that carried a similar penalty in civilian life, such as murder. They have argued that in a considerable number of cases there was an inadequate defence because of lack of experience in the defending officer, or a lack of information made known to the court, or no account taken of medical evidence, or little value given to personal or family circumstance. There seems to be little consistency in which men had their sentences commuted — some eleven percent of men sentenced to death were actually executed. These other sentences reached the level of the farcical, given the nature of the original judgement and sentence. Dr Alf Peacock, the editor of *Gunfire*, tells me that in one case the death sentence was commuted to five days confined to barracks!

Sub Lieutenant Edwin Dyett

The reasons for the rigorous use of the death sentence has been justified by its defenders as being to support the morale of the army, by showing the consequences of an action, or a failure of what was perceived to be duty. It might be necessary because of problems within a particular battalion (other armies just extinguished the complete record of a Regiment and dispersed its personnel in cases of such dishonour). It might be (as in the forty or so cases of murder) that the sentence was the equivalent to what civilian society would have awarded.

The end result of all of this publicity is that the courts martial files, closed originally for one hundred years, have now been opened for perusal at the Public Records Office. Some are still clamouring for a pardon for all of those executed, on the grounds that they were denied rudimentary justice. To my mind this sets dangerous precedents, and in any case, begs the question of where is there an end to it? Should men in the Boer and Crimean Wars be pardoned? What of the many executed in Wellington's armies for crimes as paltry as pinching some chickens? What of children being hung in the nineteenth century for what we should now regard as miniscule crimes against property — and in many cases equally poorly defended, and in our own lights equally unjustly sentenced. Finally, if one pardons them all, this takes no account of those who were vicious murderers and were *tried fairly within the law and the norms of justice as they then stood.*

One of the veterans with whom I have talked on this matter was remarkably unsympathetic towards those who were executed — we had to go up the line, we had to face the shelling and mayhem, they opted out, would be an imprecise and rather generalised summary of his views. The Australian Army, to the displeasure not only of Haig, was not subject to the death sentence. This arguably produced the worst discipline record of any part of the British and Dominion Armies, and far worse so than their immediate Dominion neighbours, New Zealand. On the other hand, the Anzacs along with the Canadians and a few select British Divisions were the finest fighting troops in the British Empire's war effort.

Enough of modern controversy; I think no-one can deny that many of the courts martial were flawed. Suffice it to say that no British soldier was executed in the Second World War for offences against Military Discipline.

One of the most celebrated of these cases, even during the war, was that relating to an officer of the Royal Naval Division (the

63rd), Sub Lieutenant Edwin Dyett of the Nelson Battalion. The officer was shot in January 1917 for an offence that was committed during the Battle of the Ancre in November 1916. The matter of the iniquities of the trial were brought to public prominence by Horatio Bottomley's *John· Bull*, an early example of tabloid journalism. Subsequent investigations have shown that what was written had a very limited connection with the facts, but there was enough evidence for unease to result in questions being asked in the House of Commons in February 1918.

One of the great works of Great War literature is AP Herbert's, *The Secret Battle*, published in 1919, and several times subquently, earning an introduction in the 1928 edition by Winston Churchill, and more recently by John Terraine in the Oxford University Press edition of 1982. This short book has as its theme justice. It opens, "I am going to write down some of the history of Harry Penrose, because I do not think full justice has been done to him, and because there must be many other young men of his kind who flung themselves into this war at the beginning of it, and have gone out of it after many sufferings with the unjust and ignorant condemnation of their fellows." The book ends, "This book is not an attack on any person, on the death penalty, or on anything else, though if it makes people think about these things, so much the better. I think I believe in the death penalty — I do not know. But I did not believe in Harry getting shot.
That is the gist of it; that my friend Harry was shot for cowardice — and he was one of the bravest men I ever knew."

Dyett was the only member of the 63rd Division to be shot during the war, and therefore the only personal contact that AP

A P Herbert with his men in the winter of 1916, at rest on the Somme resort of St Valery.

Herbert is likely to have had with such a case (and Herbert, even then, was a member of Hawke Battalion). There is no doubt that Penrose and Dyett are not the same men — there are similarities, but very little to do with their actual war service. Whatever the truth of this matter, it seems that the case of Dyett produced some, if not all, of Herbert's reaction to the courts martial procedures. What he did write was one of those eloquent historical novels based in many cases on personal experience, and which places it in the same league as Williamson's *Chronicles of Sunlit Years* and Manning's *Middle Part of Fortune*.

For a guide to the Battlefields this section on Dyett is somewhat out of place: how can a guide recreate psychological conditions within an individual, or the pressures that surrounded him? Nevertheless, the events that were to lead to his death at Le Crotoy took place here, at the time in the vile conditions of a mud bath in bleak November weather. Dyett had been kept in reserve by his Commanding Officer, who was himself a casualty in the subsequent attack. The Nelson Battalion was in the second wave of attack, on the middle right of the Division front. Dyett claimed to get lost when he was sent forward with a party of reinforcements and they eventually took shelter in a dugout. The battle was a particularly fierce and hard fought one, the Division suffering over four thousand casualties. Subsequently he met up with a staff officer who was collecting stragglers on the battlefield, and ordered him to follow and to watch out for anyone who might fall out. Dyett wished to return to Brigade HQ for fresh orders as he thought that the situation was so chaotic (which indeed it most certainly was) that instructions might well be changed. The staff officer knew Dyett, and was said to have disliked Dyett from their training days at the outbreak of war. In due course Dyett was reported for disobeying an order, and he was found in a nearby village two days later.

After the Battle of the Ancre, the severely mauled Naval Division was withdrawn to the sea, in and around the village of St Firmin near the estuary of the Somme. Dyett spent weeks waiting — he was 'sick of waiting' — for some conclusion to be reached about his actions on November 13th. The General Court Martial took place on Boxing Day at Ferme du Champ Neuf, and the panel of judges consisted of commanders who had fought on the battlefield, probably presided over by a Brigadier General.

Dyett did not offer himself as a witness in his own defence, and indeed that defence largely rested on Dyett's very nervous state

and the fact that he had requested a transfer for service at sea —
in short that he was neurotic and unfit for Active Service.

Dyett was sentenced to death by the court, but with a
recommendation for mercy on the usual grounds of youth (he was
just twenty one at the time of the battle) but also, as Sykes and
Putkowski observe, "more interestingly, that the prevailing
conditions on the day of the battle were likely to have had a
detrimental effect on any but the strongest of young men."

As has been described earlier in this book, Major General Shute
was far from being the most popular of Divisional commanders,
and in past years he has been accused of supporting the execution,
but in fact he supported the court's recommendation. The Corps
and Army Commanders, Generals Fanshawe and Gough both
maintained that the sentence should stand. This would leave Haig
as the last hope, and he generally intervened at this stage either
because of the recommendations of subordinate formation
commanders, or on the advice of the Judge Advocate General's
department at GHQ.

Dyett, as indeed most involved in the case, had anticipated a
punishment such as loss of his commission and reduction to the
ranks. The custom was that the notification of sentence was not
made until a short time before the execution, which took place
on January 5th 1917 almost certainly in the vicinity of the farm
where Dyett had been under house arrest and been tried. He is
buried in a Communal cemetery in the small seaside resort of Le

**Ferme du Champ Neuf, the scene of Dyett's imprisonment, trial and — probably —
of his subsequent execution.**

Crotoy, in a plot where there are French as well as British, and victims of both the Great and Second World War. Other unusual aspects of the case are discussed more fully in the books cited, both being readily available. However one that is in neither book is the fact that the Admiralty had issued no Death Certificate for Edwin Dyet — it being their responsibility so to do; in fact it took some persistence in recent years to get this final page of Edwin Dyett's life completed. It describes the cause of death as being, 'War Service'.

It is a pleasant enough journey along the valley of the Somme to the little seaport of Le Crotoy, with its narrow streets and resort atmosphere. On the far side of the estuary is the port, St Valery, from which William the Conqueror set sail to begin his conquest of England. The journey to Dyett's last resting place and a knowledge of something of the history of this young man who had been commissioned in June 1915 can only make us think how varied are the victims of the degeneration of human values and judgement that is a consequence of war.

Le Crotoy Communal Cemetery.

HERE WE ARE AGAIN — TRENCH RAID, 8th JUNE 1918.

The view of the attack of the 7/East Yorks is probably best seen from the western lip of the Hawthorn Crater; that of the 6/Dorsets from the Newfoundland Park near Y Ravine and from the track that runs around to the west of it. Dispositions are clearly marked out on the map.

See Map 12

I consider this raid to have been very well prepared and carried out, and reflects great credit on the two Battalions.
13.6.18   J. Byng, General [commanding Third Army]

The spring of 1918 was a perilous one for the allies. The Germans launched a series of offensives on the Western Front, known collectively as the Ludendorff Offensive. In the area of the Somme, where the initial blow had been struck in late March 1918, the fighting brought the two sides back over the heavy fighting of 1916, and at Beaumont Hamel back to the trench positions of July 1st.

When the Germans failed to break through to Amiens, they switched their attention to Flanders; this attack was also to fail. But to the British it was far from clear that the German attack was over — they still had numerous divisions freed from the fighting on the Eastern Front (peace with Bolshevik Russia was signed at Brest-Litovsk in March 1918) — and no one knew where the next blow would come.

The 17th Division had ended up on the banks above the Ancre in the April of 1918. On May 27th they moved back into the line about Beaumont Hamel on the same day that the Germans launched their offensive against the French and some severely weakened British divisions in the area around Rheims. All was relatively quiet, then, for the men of the 17th (Northern) Division, enjoying a good summer in Picardy.

On the 4th June the Germans launched a raid on the brigade facing the Beaumont Hamel defences. It was short (ten minute occupation of the British trenches) and sharp; three strong parties entered the British trenches after a short 'hurricane' barrage that commenced at 2.30 am. The Germans succeeded in killing ten British troops, wounding twenty eight others and carrying off fifteen prisoners — or at least, fifteen men were posted as missing. The Germans made good their withdrawal, leaving no dead or wounded behind to be identified. It was an efficient and clinical raid.

Map12. Trench raid 8 June, 1918

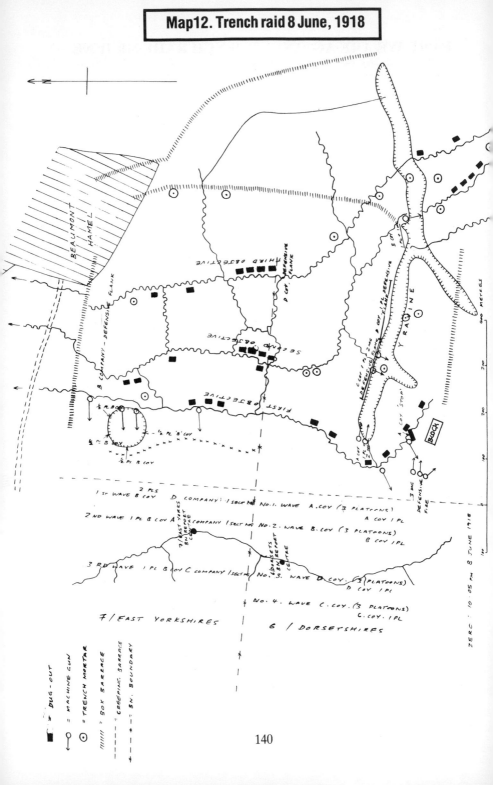

BEAUMONT HAMEL

THIRD OBJECTIVE

SECOND OBJECTIVE

FIRST OBJECTIVE

B COMPANY - DEFENSIVE FLANK

D COY. DEFENSIVE FLANK

RAVINE

C COY. 1/2 2ND... DEFENSIVE FLANK

D COY.1/2 2ND DEFENSIVE FLANK

A COY STOP

BLOCK

A COY DEFENSIVE FLEE

3 MG

½ PL 'B' COY.

½ PL 'B' COY.

½ PL B COY

2 PLS
1ST WAVE B COY   D COMPANY ISECT   No.1. WAVE   A.COY (3 PLATOONS)
                                                                    A COY 1 PL

7/EAST YORKS BN. REPORT CTRE

2ND WAVE 1 PL B COY A COMPANY ISECT   No.2. WAVE   B.COY (3 PLATOONS)
                                                                    B COY 1 PL

3 RD WAVE 1 PL B COY C COMPANY ISECT   No. 3. WAVE D.COY. (3 PLATOONS)
                                                                    D COY 1 PL

6/DORSETS BN. REPORT CENTRE

                                       No. 4. WAVE C.COY. (3 PLATOONS)
                                                                    C.COY. 1 PL

7/EAST YORKSHIRES   6 / DORSETSHIRES

ZERO : 10·05 PM 8 JUNE 1918

900 METRES   300   200   100   0   100

= DUG - OUT
= MACHINE GUN
= TRENCH MORTAR
= BOX BARRAGE
= CREEPING BARRAGE
= BN. BOUNDARY

140

50 Brigade, under the command of Brigadier General Gwynn Thomas had already been planning a large scale raid of their own; this was to be the biggest of its type attempted by the 17th Division. The objective of the raid was 'to kill Germans, secure identifications, destroy defences and demolish dugouts'. It was to cover the area of the front running from the north (or left) of the Hawthorn Ridge mine crater to the left (northern) bank of Y Ravine, a front of about five hundred yards and was to go to a depth of some four hundred yards, getting through to the third line of German trenches.

This raid was to be one in force; the attack was to be by eighteen officers and five hundred men from both 7/East Yorks and 6/Dorsets — a total of over a thousand men in the attack. They were to be supported by a range of artillery from heavy howitzers to 18 pounders — 107 artillery pieces in all. These would provide both a creeping and a box barrage. The box barrage would cut off the Germans in the selected attack area from both reinforcement and retreat; the creeping barrage would keep them in their dugouts whilst the attackers advanced as closely behind it as they could. In addition to the artillery, the attacking force had the support of 35 trench mortars and the huge number of 96 Vickers machine guns.

The two attacking battalions came out of the line on June 1st, and returned to their billets at Acheux Wood. From late on 2nd June they practised their respective battalion drills for the attack; on 4th June, under the eagle eyes of their Brigade and Divisional (Major General Robertson) commanders, the battalions rehearsed the raid together over the practise ground on the west of the Acheux-Bertrancourt Road. Other arrangements included the issuing of maps of the ground to all Officers and NCOs, and the entire attacking force went to a 'lantern slide' exhibition showing aerial photographs of the raid area. Specialist sections were chosen to be trained in explosive techniques by Royal Engineers, and witnessed various 'live' demonstrations, to ensure that German dugouts were efficiently destroyed. On 6th June the battalions individually and then together rehearsed the raid. On 7th June they had a quiet day, carrying out final preparations, before moving up to the line at 9.30 pm. As many men as possible were concealed in dugouts, and the outward appearance of a low profile was maintained throughout the day of 8th June. A large number of gaps (some forty) were cut in the British wire, and a white board was placed in the trenches opposite each gap indicating exit routes to the troops.

Zero was at 10.05 pm.

7/East Yorks had the following targets for its attacking companies. Each company was some one hundred and twenty strong, each company consisting of four platoons.

'D Coy (1st Wave) will attack, capture and destroy the 1st German Objective [ie German front line].

A Coy (2nd Wave) will pass through 1st and 2nd objectives [ie German front and second line of trenches], push straight forward closely behind creeping barrage & capture & destroy the 3rd Objective [ie third line of German trenches]. They will push out covering patrols & LGs [Lewis guns] as close to final barrage as possible.

C Coy (3rd wave) will follow A Coy through the 1st Objective to the 2nd Objective & will capture & destroy the latter.

B Coy (1st wave) will take & mop up the CRATER with the trenches on the Eastern Lip with two platoons advancing closely under the barrage. One half platoon will attack CRATER frontally, one half platoon will enter it from the NORTHERN edge, one half platoon will enter it from the Southern edge and one half platoon will enter the trench behind from the NORTHERN edge, and join hands with D Coy.

The platoon of B Coy with each of the 2nd & 3rd Waves will advance with their respective waves to protect the left flank throughout.'

In addition, there was a section of the Battalion HQ Lewis gunners attached to each wave to guard the right flank of the attack (ie that part adjoining the 6/Devons), whilst another section was to be rushed forward to the northern lip of the crater to guard the left flank if it was thought to be necessary.

The narrative of what actually happened is simple and straightforward.

'ZERO was 10.5 pm & 30 seconds before this hour & before the artillery really opened out, our Machine Gunners commenced

Panorama from near the German Front Line on Hawthorn Ridge.

Hawthorn Ridge No 1   The Sunken Road/   The Crater
                              Hunter's Lane

putting down their barrage. The sections rapidly filed through the gaps, lined up outside the wire & each wave shook out into its two lines as they moved forward. The enemy barrage came down at ZERO + 1 minute on our Front line & Support but all troops had got quite clear & missed the barrage entirely. They moved straight up to the [British] barrage & under its protection went to the attack. The 1st Wave entered and captured the 1st Objective at ZERO plus five minutes thirty seconds & the other two waves moved through them closely following the barrage, the 2nd WAVE going straight ON to the 3rd Objective. There was some slight delay in getting onto the 3rd Objective in the centre owing to the Artillery barrage remaining too long on this point, otherwise the whole raid went absolutely like clockwork. All objectives were gained, Lewis guns were pushed out in front of the final objectives & close up under stationary Protective [Box] Barrage and Lewis Rifles (sic) were also disposed in depth on the outside of the Left Flank, each objective having one L.G. on its left flank with one in front and 3 L.G.s took up flank positions between our Front Line & 1st Objective.

At ZERO + 50 minutes a signal of a volley of 12 green Very lights was sent up by my orders & the companies from the 1st and 2nd objectives withdrew according to plan. This signal was further helped by a Bugler sounding a "G" on his bugle upon the signal [this was done, presumably, to prevent any confusion that might be caused by the Germans coincidentally firing similar coloured flares].

The 1st Objective was held until all troops in front had passed back & at ZERO plus 80 minutes a signal of a volley of 12 white Very lights was sent up by my orders, upon which a Bugler again sounded a "G" & the troops withdrew and reoccupied our original Front Line and held until relieved by troops of the 51st Brigade who were in readiness.'

7/East Yorks suffered eighty casualties in the attack, and given

German Stronghold
November 13th

Beaumont
Hamel
Church

its scale this was 'acceptable'. They captured 28 Germans, killed or wounded many more. The report states, rather ominously, 'A good number more were captured, but on the way back they became obstinate & were dealt with.' Their fate does not require much imagination. The Battalion captured machine guns, destroyed some trench mortars and their emplacements, six dugouts were bombed and then completely destroyed and others were set on fire by the use of phosphorous bombs.

As far as the CO, Lt Col Gilbert East King, DSO, was concerned, the 'chief result is that the morale of our attacking troops, many of whom are latest recruits & have never been over before, has been raised to the highest pitch, & they treat the fighting Hun with supreme contempt.' This was despite the fact that the prisoners, 'were all of good physique and were of 1st class type. They were very quiet and very subdued.' The CO was to get a DSO for his efforts; his citation in the London Gazette for 24th

The Trench Raid – perhaps as it was hoped that they would turn out!

September reads: "For conspicuous gallantry and devotion to duty during a raid made by two battalions into the enemy's lines. His utter disregard for personal danger, skill and cheerfulness throughout, inspired all under his command and proved him to be a leader of a high order. Throughout the raid he remained exposed to enemy fire in an advanced position which would enable him to control the operations, which he did extremely well. It was due to his indomitable example that his battalion was imbued with a fighting spirit which nothing could daunt.'

The story of 6/Dorsets is broadly similar, although they faced a more complex problem — the infamous Y Ravine. It was outside the scope of the Raid proper, but its defences, and the potential for the Germans to use it as a rallying point and a springboard for a counter-attack, meant that considerable precautions to guard the right flank had to be made These are illustrated on the map. The raid was a 'great success — the Battalion killing many Germans in hand to hand fighting, capturing about forty prisoners and 4 machine guns.' The Battalion suffered over 150 casualties, of whom thirty or so were killed, a large number of which had to be left behind the German lines. One of those who survived was Capt GT Morris, commanding D Company. Soon after the company went over the top, he was seen to go to ground. A voice called out, 'The Captain's hit', to which he replied, 'The captain isn't hit, he's dropped his pipe!' Two officers, 2/Lts EJ Leate and LW Forde, were killed — they are commemorated on the Pozieres Memorial. They were members of B Coy, whose objective was the final one, the German third line of trenches. It was in this area that the bulk of the Dorsets casualties took place. Several of those killed in the action, including one of the 'originals', Sgt WT Gerrard, were buried at Acheux Military Cemetery.

The battalion won numerous awards for the action (although the CO was not to get a DSO until 1919); two bars to MCs, three MCs, one DCM and thirteen MMs. The Regimental history commented, 'It was fierce and murderous work of not an hour's duration: one of three definite occasions when blood was hot for killing, and the Dorsets showed their fangs in real anger and slew their enemies face to face.' It was estimated that some one hundred and fifty Germans were killed. The heavy casualties that the battalion suffered were largely due to German gunfire from the right. It meant that the Medical Officer had a busy time in the aid post — by the end of it he was covered in blood.

At 8 am the officers of the battalions gathered together with their Brigadier at Acheux for eggs and bacon, coffee and rum in place of the hoped for champagne, which failed to materialise.

The raid was important — it helped to dispel the notion that German troops (and those facing the 17th Division were good) were invincible, and it marked a return to the attack; although expensive in casulaties, the planning had gone very well in execution, and the large number of new drafts that had come out since the March Retreat had been bloodied in a successful action.

There were fears over the next days that the Germans would be launching a further assault in the Somme area; but nothing materialised. In fact for some weeks both the British and German armies suffered from the epidemic of influenza that was to have such fatal consequences for many of the civilian populations of Europe. The tide began to turn against the Germans when the French launched the first of a series of counter-attacks on the Marne; whilst the 17th Division began its own part in the great Advance to Victory on August 21st. As far as the men of 7/East Yorks and 6/Dorsets were concerned, their 'advance' had begun on June 8 1918.

Late August 1918 was to be the last time that the village — the pulverised remnant — of Beaumont Hamel was to feature in the communiques of the Great War.

THE CEMETERIES AND THE MEMORIALS

1 and 2. MESNIL RIDGE CEMETERY AND KNIGHTSBRIDGE CEMETERY

These cemeteries are very difficult of access. The road to them is indicated by a CWGC sign on the western outskirts of Mesnil; like so many of the small roads in the Somme area, it promises well. However, it is not long before the surface progressively degenerates, from a metalled surface to a good track, to a hair-raising experience when the sump seems to be likely to be an early casualty! I have done it by car, but I would recommend that as soon as you feel that the going is getting tough that you stop there and make the rest of your way by foot. See Maps 3, 14

To the left of the track for much of the way the line of the old Albert — Doullens light railway (which existed prior to the war) may be discerned — there was a station in Mesnil, to the immediate south west of where the turn to the cemeteries is made. After some distance Knightsbridge Cemetery may be seen to the right; Mesnil Ridge Cemetery is on the other side of the old railway line, to the left.

The cemeteries are situated on a featureless piece of ground. Mesnil Ridge Cemetery is small, with only ninety five burials in it. It is unusual in that all but one of those buried here is identified. It is a battlefield cemetery: that is that the men were buried here at the time of their death; concentration cemeteries were created by (in general) either extending an existing cemetery or by creating a new one by bringing in the dead who had been buried in small or scattered plots from the vicinity, or on occasion from further afield. Mesnil Ridge Cemetery was created by Field Ambulances and units mainly in the 36th (Ulster) Division and then the 29th Division from August 1915 to August 1916. Presumably the Field

Mesnil Ridge Cemetery, with the trackway of the old light railway to the right.

Ambulances were making use of the almost imperceptible fold in the ground to offer some shelter and the track of the light railway to provide a means of evacuation of the wounded. A number of the casualties of the raid on Mary Redan (all those here from 2/South Wales Borderers), referred to in the chapter on the Newfoundland Regiment, found their resting place here. There is only one casualty from the Newfoundland Regiment in this cemetery: Private George Curnew was killed by a bullet which struck him on April 24th whilst he was working on the parapet in the front line. It was the first fatality in France, the first time the regiment had entered the front line since they had arrived from Gallipoli and only one week since the unfortunate Private Curnew had joined the battalion with a small draft. He is buried in Row F Grave 1.

Knightsbridge Cemetery is much the bigger of the two, opening when the Battle of the Somme began, and used by units whenever this area found itself in the battle zone — in 1916 and early 1917 and for a few months in 1918. Most of those buried straight in front, and to the right, of the cemetery entrance were brought in from the neighbourhood after the armistice. It is situated just to the west of the site of a communication trench, Knightsbridge Barracks which ran south of the car park of the Newfoundland Park. Amongst the men of the Newfoundland Regiment buried here is one of the Ayre cousins. Right at the end of Row B lie a group of eight officers of the 4/Bedfords, which was a part of 190 Brigade (63rd Division). They were all killed on November 13th, as their battalion advanced in support of the attack, possibly victims of the strongpoint in the German first line that caused so much trouble to the British on that day.

Knightsbridge Cemetery looking across to the Newfoundland Memorial Park, signified by the trees and the coach in the car park.

Auchonvillers Military Cemetery, looking across to the farm which was the site of the Collecting Post in the November attack.

3. AUCHONVILLERS MILITARY CEMETERY

This cemetery can be easily missed; it is set well back from the road, and is approached by a track on the right hand side of the Auchonvillers-Mailly road just after the last farm building in Auchonvillers. This farm is the site of the Collecting Post mentioned in 'Saving the Wounded'. It was natural that the dead should be buried nearby, and the cemetery is almost a chronological record of the units that served in this sector of the front. From here there are good views across the country to Mailly Maillet, over the ground across which so many men passed for their last time in the bloody months of late 1916. Like so many of the Battlefield cemeteries, it has very few unidentified; under ten percent of the total, and of those a significant proportion are amongst the fifteen concentrated here after the armistice.

4. AUCHONVILLERS COMMUNAL CEMETERY

Besides the cemeteries that were built for the casualties of the war, a large number of 'communal' cemeteries were used by all sides during the conflict. Usually the War Graves Commission put a small green plaque on or near the cemetery gates (for those with

149

only a few British buried there) to indicate the fact that there are Commonwealth burials in that cemetery. Since there are so few (the larger numbers of burials in a Communal are usually buried in what is described as an 'extension') buried in these cemeteries there is rarely a register in place, and one has to hope that it is included in a neighbouring British cemetery. In this case the details are to be found in Auchonvillers Military Cemetery.

There are fifteen British soldiers buried in this cemetery, thirteen of them in 1/Border who were killed by a hurricane bombardment of a communication trench (Second Avenue) on 6 April 1916. There is also buried here one of the earlier superintendents of the Newfoundland Park; he has a CWGC type headstone and it is obvious that the grave is maintained by them.

The red coloured headstones were part of an experiment by the War Graves to find a long lasting stone (especially, but by no means exclusively, for use in these small plots) which could stand up to the ravages of the weather and not require the constant cleaning that the traditional stone has needed.

5. 'Y' RAVINE CEMETERY
The cemetery register is often a great source of knowledge, sometimes of a surprising type. This cemetery register tells the reader that Beaumont Hamel has been adopted by Winchester — a common practice after the war, as the towns and villages of the war-ravaged areas tried to recover from the cataclysm that had reduced them to being described as 'ruins' on maps. Sheffield, for example, adopted Serre and Birmingham took on Albert, which explains the Rue Birmingham that runs alongside the Basilica.

Y Ravine Cemetery

This is a concentration cemetery, like so many in this vicinity, created by the V Corps burial officer after the battle had moved on from here in the spring of 1917. It is situated just to the south of the fork of Y Ravine, which itself ran in a south westerly direction from the main ravine. It is no longer possible to see this fork, as part of it has been landscaped into a field; but there is quite clearly a bank remaining, which enables the position to be located. The cemetery is in No Man's Land, and access is usually through the Newfoundland Park, within whose boundaries the cemetery stands.

Just under fifty percent of the burials are unidentified. Amongst those whose name is known is CSM Joseph Fairbrass of 2/South Wales Borderers, who fell on July 1st. He saw service at Gallipoli and was one of six brothers who served, three of whom were killed during the war.

The cemetery is a good place from which to survey the German position and their viewpoint of the British attack — this is why the cemetery is included on the map of the Newfoundland attack, so that readers may get their bearings.

The closely packed graves of Hawthorn Ridge Number 2 betray its origins as a concenration cemetery.

6. HAWTHORN RIDGE CEMETERY NO. 2

Another concentration cemetery, this also is the work of V Corps. The open nature of the cemetery layout perhaps indicated more clearly than in other similar places that the cemetery was created specifically for burying a large number of dead simultaneously. In essence it consisted of two long trenches and the dead would, presumably, have been packed in together as closely as possible. One can almost imagine the scene of the burial officer matching bodies to names, ordering them to be put in the trench, a burial service for all of them and then covering the lot up. The packed nature of the burials is indicated not only by the fact that the headstones have no spaces between them, but also that more than one name appears frequently on the one stone; when they came from more than one regiment the War Graves came up with the strangely moving solution of having the two cap badges interlinked.

It is worthwhile mentioning here that V Corps were not the first to clear this battlefield; after the relative success of the November 1916 attack large numbers of the dead of July 1st were removed from the battlefield and were buried in the rear areas, in cemeteries such as that at Mailly Maillet.

The much smaller front row consists chiefly of those who were concentrated to this cemetery after the armistice.

7. HUNTER'S CEMETERY

This small cemetery (another one by V Corps) was created by using a large shell hole to create a mass burial; many of those who lie buried here were members of the 6 and 7/Black Watch which attacked this side of the Y Ravine in November 1916. It is also characteristic of the care that the War Graves Commission took in designing the cemeteries so that individuality could be expressed and that the final resting places would not just be a series of uninspired burial plots.

The register proclaims that the origin of the name of the cemetery is unknown; Martin Middlebrook suggests that it might be taken from the company commander who organised the burial of the dead; it might also come from Hunter's Trench, which incorporated the infamous Sunken Road just to the west of Beaumont Hamel.

Just behind the cemetery, under the ground, is a network of tunnels and dug outs that have been rediscovered recently. Steve Austin Senior, who was Superintendent of the Park for many years, was aware of these tunnels, but on discovering that his son, Steve Austin Junior, had been discovered playing around them when a child, had the entrances filled in. Recent land slippage (1993) has revealed some of these entrances once more. Whilst interesting, I hope that it is quite clear to everyone how extremely unsafe these tunnels and dug outs are — observe, wonder, but keep well clear! Steve Austin Junior has succeeded his father as Superintendent of the Park.

8. HAWTHORN RIDGE CEMETERY NO. 1

This is yet another V Corps concentration cemetery. The dead buried here are mainly from the 29th Division, and of those who have been identified over half were members of 16th (Public Schools) Battalion the Middlesex Regiment. It is signposted from the Hamel — Auchonvillers road, and also from Newfoundland Park, where access is gained from a track around the west end of Y Ravine and then a short trek across a field. It provides an excellent point from which to view British and German positions, especially before the western side of Beaumont Hamel. It is unfortunate from this point of view that the trees in Newfoundland Park make it difficult to get a true impression of the strength of the German line here.

Hawthorn Ridge No 1, with the crater to the right in the mass of bushes and undergrowth.

9. BEAUMONT HAMEL BRITISH CEMETERY

This cemetery is situated in the middle of the July 1st (and November 13th, for that matter) battlefield. The high bank on its west side is the remnant of the remblai that provided yet another hazard for the men of 1/Lancashire Fusiliers on July 1st. It was also to cause trouble for the 8th Argylls in their attack on November 13th. German wire was protected by the bank and did not get

Beaumont Hamel British cemetery at the foot of the remblai, with the German line indicated by the wood to the east (ie right hand edge of photograph).

properly broken up. The A Company of that battalion got caught up in it, and its commander, Captain Alastair Macarthur, to be followed in due course by his second in command, Lt Jack McKeller, were killed: they are buried at Mailly Wood Cemetery. The German line can be easily imagined, running around the small wood some yards to its east. The cemetery was created after the success of the November 13th attack and was used by the various units serving in this sector until February 1917, although about a fifth of the burials were concentrated here after the armistice. Amongst those buried here is 2/Lt Owen Fox, a rather elderly subaltern aged 47, who was killed in February 1917 whilst serving with 1/Dorsets. During the South African War he had been a lieutenant in the Cape Mounted Rifles, and possessed the Queen's and King's Medals with six clasps.

The view of the 1/8 Argyll and Sutherland Highlanders' memorial, the Sunken Road, this cemetery and remblai and the German line signified by the small wood, which may be had from the lip of Hawthorn Crater, collectively provides to my mind one of the moving battlefield sights on the Western Front.

10. REDAN RIDGE CEMETERY NO. 2

This is situated some hundred yards west of the old German July 1st front line. It is situated close to the boundary between the 4th and 29th divisions. All but one of those buried here were killed in July and November 1916. Many of those buried here served with 1/Hampshires, a part of the 4th Division, which helps to explain the Winchester connection with Beaumont Hamel. The village also used to have a large German concentration cemetery, but in the early 1920s most of the German dead on the Somme were concentrated to Fricourt or to Rancourt.

11. ANCRE BRITISH CEMETERY

This was another of V Corps concentration cemeteries, created in the spring of 1917. After the Armistice almost two thousand graves were concentrated here to join the five hundred or so who had been buried in Plots 3 and 4. A surprising number of relatively large war time cemeteries were concentrated These included Ancre River British Cemetery No. 2, 350 yards further along the road to Beaucourt which contained sixty four men from the 63rd Division, Beaucourt Station Cemetery, close to that station with eighty five men from the winter fighting of 1916 — 1917; Green Dump Cemetery to the south west of station road, and probably named after the Green Line, an objective for the November 13th attack, which was another cemetery used during the winter of 1916 — 1917, with forty five burials; others in the open countryside between here, Beaucourt and Beaumont Hamel — RND Cemetery with 336 burials, Sherwood Cemetery with 176 burials and Station Road Cemetery with 82 burials. Finally, there was another 'Y' Ravine Cemetery (No. 2), which was situated in the open fields to the left of Mary Redan, not far from the British front line, where 140 men were buried.

The cemetery is in a deep hollow which was firmly in No Man's Land in July 1916 but was either partly within, or just in front of, the British line on November 13th. From the top of the cemetery there are commanding views across the Ancre to the heights above, and a clear view over the ground that some of the units of the northern part of the 63rd Division attack had to cross.

Amongst the dead is the Honourable Vere Harmsworth, killed before the redoubt just above the cemetery. His father was Viscount Rothermere, proprietor of the Daily Mail. There is an interesting permanent plaque at the base of his headstone, recording a pilgrimage by Hungarian Boy Scouts to his grave in the inter-war years. The character of the early days of the Naval Division is perhaps summed up by his stone and that of Able Seaman William Brown, also of Hawke Battalion, who had learned articles published in the Philosphical Magazine in 1915 and posthumously in the Proceedings of the Royal Society of Edinburgh.

The cemetery is a quiet spot in an area which is well visited, and I have stopped here on more than one occasion to have a picnic lunch seated on the bench seats thoughtfully provided by the CWGC. The continuing work of the War Graves Commission was shown on my last visit here, when extensive work was taking place to rebuild the entrance wall, which had become dangerous because of land slippage.

Hamel Military Cemetery. Jacob's Ladder, a communication trench, ran down the slope behind it into the village.

12. HAMEL MILITARY CEMETERY

See Map 14

This cemetery does not appear on the main tour map, but is situated at the southern end of the village, on the road to Albert. It can be missed if the driver is not careful, as it is tucked off to the north side of the road. This was a battlefield cemetery (there was a dressing station in a house just south of the turning in the village to Auchonvillers) and was in use continuously through the fighting of 1916 — 1917 and again for a short while in 1918, with only a few concentrated here after the war. There are two 1919 burials — men from the Chinese Labour Corps. These men were brought to France during the war to act as labourers, and were obtained by the British Government contracting for them from Chinese War Lords. These two were likely to have died from one of two causes — Spanish 'flu (unlikely) or as a consequence of a munitions explosion. They were used widely to help to clear the battlefield of war debris, and it is not uncommon to find one or two members of this Corps buried in various British cemeteries across Flanders. If the long coastwards journey to Le Croty is made to visit the grave of Sub Lieut Dyett, then a small diversion to visit the Chinese Cemetery at Noyelles-sur-Mer is well worthwhile. It consists entirely of members of the Chinese Labour Corps (838 of them, as well as a memorial to their missing), and is sited here because their headquarters was in the fields in front of the cemetery.

Amongst the casualties of the November fighting buried here are two of the commanding officers of battalions in the Royal Naval Division. On the slope above the cemetery lay a long communication trench, Jacob's Ladder (not to be confused with the trench of the same name near Beaumont Hamel) which ran down to Hamel, coming out near the church, from Mesnil.

MEMORIALS

1. 29TH DIVISION MEMORIAL.
This memorial is immediately in front of the visitor on entering the Newfoundland Memorial Park from the car park. It sits on an artificial mound, and its chief characteristic is the red triangle that was its divisional sign.

2. THE NEWFOUNDLAND REGIMENTAL MEMORIAL
The proud caribou, the work of the English sculptor, Basil Gotto, sits on its artificially created eminence and surveys the ground over which so many men of this faraway colony were to die. This caribou is one of five placed in various locations across the Western Front, where the regiment fought major actions. The other one located on the Somme is to be found on the outskirts of Guedecourt. The selection and arrangement of the land to be purchased and the siting of the various caribou was the work of Father TF Nangle, the RC Chaplain to the Regiment in the latter years of the war. He was also Newfoundland's representative on the (then) Imperial War Graves Commission. The caribou here is the most striking of them all, forming as it does but one part of this impressive memorial to the contribution that the country made to the allied effort during the Great War. At the base of the mound is the Memorial to the Missing from Newfoundland, which includes those who served at sea as well. The Park, too, is their memorial; and the decision to purchase this land has served Newfoundland well, for in all probability no part of the Western Front is more visited now than this small part of the Somme battlefield.

Father Tom Nangle

3 AND 4. 51ST (HIGHLAND) DIVISION MEMORIALS.
The 51st Division has two memorials here. The simple cross that stands close to Y Ravine was brought here from High Wood, the scene of a less successful series of attacks in the last days of July and the first days of August 1916. It was the first time the division had fought together as a whole formation. The simple memorial was moved here because it was considered to be in safer hands.

The magnificent bronze statue of a Gordon Highlander, modelled on CSM Rowan, stands on the old German front line and stares across Y Ravine and over the ground which the division fought over and captured in November 1916. It was unveiled by Marshal Foch.

5. 1/8 ARGYLL AND SUTHERLAND HIGHLANDERS MEMORIAL

This is a huge memorial to this battalion, and is the largest to a single battalion on the Western Front. The memorial is sited very close to the location of the headquarters of the Battalion when it went into the attack on November 13th. It carries the battle honours, cap and collar badges of the battalion as well as a record of its casualties on the base of a Celtic cross.

16. 51ST DIVISION MEMORIAL, BEAUMONT HAMEL.

This is the memorial that most people miss in this area. On entering Beaumont Hamel from the west there is a confusion of road junctions. In the triangle between this road and the Rue de Montagne (known as Frontier Lane during the war) there is the metal base of a flag pole, in danger of being concealed by a tree. There is a plaque on it, explaining that it is a gift from the men of the Highland Division to the people of Beaumont Hamel. It would be fitting if it could be restored to its proper function, though the last time I was there somebody had put some flowers by it, so it is not completely forgotten.

7. ROYAL NAVAL DIVISION MEMORIAL, BEAUCOURT-SUR-ANCRE.

This is on the north east side of the road at the end of the village on the Beaumont Hamel side, just beyond the Church, which has been moved from its pre-war position. It has a simple inscription (no mention of 63rd Division here!) referring to the action of November 13 and 14 1916. Beware of traffic here, and take care with parking the car should you wish to take a closer look.

Although handsome enough, one would not think the memorial particularly prominent. The road between Beaucourt and Hamel is for the most part hemmed in by a quite steeply rising embankment, and so little impression is gained of the ground over which the Naval Divison fought. However, from just forward of the site of Mary Redan, near Newfoundland Park, the memorial is quite visible (binoculars do help, it must be admitted). It is possible, therefore, to see much of the ground over which the Naval Division fought during those tumultuous days of November 1916.

BEHIND THE LINES. A CAR TOUR BEHIND THE LINES OF BOTH SIDES.

I have included in the guide a car route around the villages to the rear of the British and German positions which housed many of the units involved in the fighting at Beaumont Hamel, when they See Map 13 were at rest or preparing for their part in the battle. I have taken Hamel as a start point.

This journey will take some time, of course much depending on how many stops are made en route, and a morning or an afternoon should be allowed for. It is a pleasant drive in its own right, and takes you through a quiet and unspoilt part of the Somme countryside.

Both views from near the top of Jacob's Ladder, just outside Mesnil. The top view over to the east includes the Ulster Tower, which may be just seen on the skyline, in the trees, to right of centre.

The bottom view shows Thiepval and the site of the *Leipzig* redoubt, a German 1 July strongpoint, readily identified by the clump of the trees on the horizon to the right of the photograph.

From here make for Mesnil Martinsart; this can be done in one of two ways: either take the road to the south out of Hamel and take the turning to the right, just beyond Hamel Military Cemetery; or, for the more adventurous, take the road from Hamel to Auchonvillers. Just as the trees of the Newfoundland Park start on your right (the track there leads to the Superintendant's house and goes on to Y Ravine cemetery), there is a narrow road heading south. Its surface is not good but my car has made the trip in the past. This route connects eventually with the direct Hamel-Mesnil road; just before it does this, on the left, was where the communications trench, Jacob's Ladder, ran down the side of the ridge towards Hamel. If it is convenient (ie if one of the numerous tractors does not put in an appearance) look across the Ancre towards the Ulster Tower. This ridge was of vital importance for their artillery spotters and for their staff observing the progress of the battle.

Mesnil War memorial: The Departure ... The Return.

Once in Mesnil take the turning by the church to the right; the village war memorial nearby is worthy of closer examination, with two plaques depicting the scene of a Poilu departing for war and his return at the end of it. Mesnil itself was full of troops coming in and out of the line, as well as a dump for all sorts of supplies. Keep on the road to Auchonvillers; several hundred yards before it comes to a T Junction there is a British observation bunker on the left hand side of the road. You need to keep your eyes peeled for it, as it is set not very high above the ground. Good views must have been available here, but shrubs and trees seem to have obscured most of them. On the right of the road one can imagine troops making their way towards communication trenches such as Tipperary Avenue — they would have been ordered off the roads by now because of the dangers of shelling, and in any case the road surface was needed for the transports.

British observation bunker on the Mesnil to Auchonvillers road; the Thiepval memorial may be seen to the left centre of the photograph, through the line of trees.

Heavy artillery sited near Englebelmer.

At the T Junction turn left towards Vitermont and Englebelmer. Vitermont took its turn as a Brigade Headquarters, and some of the heavy artillery engaged in the preliminary bombardment for the Somme was situated around Englebelmer. Turn right just before entering the villages and head for Mailly Maillet, a large village with broad streets. Mailly Maillet and Englebelmer were the other two Somme villages besides Beaumont Hamel that Winchester adopted after the war. At a road junction you will find the church, on the right hand side. During the war the local parish priest had the facade of the west door covered in sandbags to protect it from shell fire, and thus it is a miraculous fifteenth century survival, with its beautiful carvings. Pollution would appear to be a greater threat than the enemy's shellfire.

At the junction turn left, passing a walled wooded area on your left. Immediately at the end of this there is a sign to Mailly Wood Cemetery. This is worth a detour. The track is fine until it turns to the right to the cemetery; my advice would be to walk from here. In these fields there would have been encampments housing the troops. The cemetery itself is full of many of the casualties of the Highland Division — serried ranks of them.

Mailly Wood cemetery, with serried ranks of Highland Division casualties from their attck in November 1916.

Returning to the road turn left and within half a kilometre or so take a right fork to Beaussart and Bertrancourt. Here take the road to Acheux, but just as you come out of the village take a right turn (which has a CWGC signpost to Bertrancourt Military Cemetery). The cemetery is at the end of a long grass path on the left hand side of the road, so it is necessary to be alert — one can drive past it, and the last time I visited the final (and vital!) CWGC sign was languishing in a ditch and almost completely covered by branches and vegetation.

Bertrancourt Cemetery on the left, Acheux Wood in the distance.

The cemetery was used by Dressing Stations which were in the adjacent fields during the Somme battle. Standing at the end of the cemetery, looking towards Acheux, gives a view across the fields where many of the rehearsals were done by units preparing for the various attacks in the Beaumont Hamel area. Like many of these Somme villages, Bertrancourt's larger houses would have been commandeered for various HQs — for example 4 Division and 12 Division had their headquarters here at various times during the Somme battle

Returning on the road towards Acheux, the great bulk of Acheux Wood appears on the left hand side. It was in here that the tanks were brought in the preparations for the Battle of the Ancre, by means of the railway which ran around its south eastern side and the line of which may still be traced today. The wood would have provided cover for the tanks from prying German airmen's view. Also in Acheux, but tucked well out of prying eyes, is the chateau which housed 29th Division HQ (and its Casualty Clearing Station) in its time on the Beaumont Hamel sector. It was to Acheux that the remnants of 1/Lancashire Fusiliers returned on July 4th. In Acheux head towards Herrisart (on the D114); after about five hundred yards there is a sign indicating Acheux British Cemetery. It is tucked well back from the road, on the right hand side, and is rarely visited. There are three casualties from the 6/Dorset raid of June 1918 buried here. The ground in this vicinity would seem

The rarely visited Acheux British cemetery. Rehearsals for the 1 July attack took place on the ridged ground beyond the cemetery.

to provide some similarity to that around Beaumont Hamel, and may well have been used in the pre-push preparations.

Continuing along the D114, turn right in due course for Louvencourt; this was the home for the months preceding July 1st for the Newfoundland Regiment. Before reaching the village, Louvencourt Military Cemetery will be found on the right. There are very unusual (and very impressive) French headstones here, but most visitors come to pay tribute to Brigadier General C Prowse, killed on July 1st at the Quadrilateral, now the site of Serre Road Cemetery No. 2. Also buried here is Roland Leighton, who figures prominently in Vera Britten's *Testament of Youth*. He was sniped in the trenches close to the present site of Touvent Farm, to the north west of Serre.

Louvencourt was the site chosen as a reserve area for the 88th Brigade, the reserve brigade of 29th Division. It was from here, in the relatively uneventful weeks of April and early May, that members of the Newfoundland Regiment who had not already had leave in Cairo en route to France from Gallipoli were able to go for eight days to the United Kingdom on leave. Others were not so lucky, and were called on to help build a railway line at Lealvillers (to the south), or to engage on endless route marches over the ghastly pave of the roads — the cobbles and the ammunition boots of the soldiers did not go well together. There was also extensive training in anti-gas warfare and tests were made to ensure that gas masks fitted and were effective. Whilst in the line, Englebelmer became the reserve area for the battalion; at that stage in the war it was more or less in one piece. Besides taking their place in the line, the Regiment had to provide work parties — and in the early days this was largely centred on the construction, improvement and maintenance of the Tipperary Avenue communication trench.

The Regiment spent thirty four days in total at Louvencourt, and became very attached to its inhabitants — it seems to have been a mutual feeling. Once it became clear what the role of the Regiment was to be on July 1st, the battalion began systematic training in an area to the north of Louvencourt, in the fields to the right of the road to Authie. There were frequent practices over the ground which was topographically similar and which had been marked out clearly on the ground by furrows. Many a farmer on the Somme did rather well out of the compensation paid by the British Government for the damage done to his crops by the rehearsals going on up and down behind the British line. The training was exhausting and exhaustive, involved long marches (ten miles in full fighting order was not unusual), and the Brigade staff was keen that every eventuality should be catered for, no matter how small, and rehearsed again and again. In between times the Regiment still had to provide work parties and to man the front line. By now the 29th Division was digging its own deep dugouts near the front to hold hundreds of men; building bridges across trenches that would be able to carry Horse Artillery; cutting zig-zag paths through their own wire, and providing carrying parties — never-ending carrying parties — to bring endless trench stores to dumps: screw pickets, coils of wire, timber, petrol tins filled with water, duckboards, pit props and, most dreaded of all, toffee apple mortar bombs and gas cylinders. The experience of the Newfoundland Regiment on the Somme in the months prior to the great attack was no different to that of the tens of battalions preparing for the Big Push.

It is worth stopping the car and taking a short stroll around Louvencourt — it has massive houses and farms and barns that the soldiers of so long ago might have no difficulty in recognising — indeed they might well be survivors, judging from the rickety appearance and rather old-fashioned method of construction.

For the return journey head straight for Acheux and then Forceville. The Hood Battalion of the Royal Naval Division spent some time billeted here in the early days of October 1916. From there take the minor road to Mailly Maillet, passing to the north of another huge wood.

The 1/8 Argyll and Sutherland Highlanders passed this way

(along with the rest of their brigade) from their billets in Forceville en route to their positions for the attack on November 13th. The anonymous chronicler of that battalion describes the preparations and the move up on November 12th, which here follows, in an edited form.

'Some platoons are being served out with bombs, two per man — others are drawing picks and shovels to be used for making fire-steps on the eastern side of the enemy trenches, after they are taken. (There is no question of their not being taken although shell holes near the front line are inhabited by skeletons of troops that did fail). Many individuals are busy sewing on their tunics the four vertical red bars, which distinguish the 8th Argylls from other battalions in the division — and yet others write home, which may be their last, yet are filled with a spirit of optimism which can hardly fail to cheer the recipients at home.

'The general feeling is one of elation. The anticipation of exchanging the monotony of "holding the line" for the adventure of crossing No Man's Land and getting in a shrewd blow at the Boches, causes a pleasurable excitement. They feel that they are going to help to shorten the war. Individually, underlying this elation and pride, there may be occasionally a melancholy qualm that one may get killed or crippled. It is a qualm which arrives at odd moments, and which soon passes away in the stir which is going on. Some there are, unfortunately, who know (as far as human beings can foretell the future) that they are going to be killed. Maybe it is that "fey" state to which Highland people are subject. A few show it in their demeanour, however bravely they may try to hide it. Poor lads! Their time of great trial is now, not in the hectic moments of the attack.

Darkness begins to fall. The order, "Estaminets are all out of bounds" increases the general excitement. Then the command, "Fall in at 9 pm." comes as a welcome finale to the weeks of waiting for the great day in prospect. At 9 pm platoons are falling in — hard to see them in the darkness, as they line up around the dung heaps in the courtyard of the little farms where they are billeted. Platoon sergeants call the roll quietly — subalterns make a quick inspection of equipment, then out through the archway into the road to take their position in battalion in line of march. Formal orders are few. Each company simply tacks itself on to the rear of the Company it has been detailed to follow — and similarly with regard to the battalions. (The 8th Argyll's left Forceville with 21 officers and 674 other ranks.) They take their place in the brigade line of march at the appointed time. The word passes back, "No smoking" a hefty jolt to the lad that loves his Woodbine! No smell of fragrant smoke to inspire him as he stumbles along that dark Forceville-Mailly Maillet road, ankle deep in mud — nothing to see in the darkness, except the dim outline of the man in front with the points of his pick sticking out on either side of his head like a pair of horns! Not inspiring this, makes one think of another world, where shovels are, according to report, in common use. The march also is the very worst of its kind; it cannot be properly called a march, but merely a stumble or succession of stumbles. Stumble fifty yards — stop — "What's up?". "Something in front". Stumble another fifty — another stop — same question — same reply, and so on for hours. And that equipment! Quite light and comfortable when one first puts it on the back there in Forceville, but now getting heavier and heavier with every step. Comfortable it was too, but now developing as many points as there are on the compass! One gets one's fingers under the strap, gives a heave upwards to throw the haversack on the back of the neck — and stumbles on again. Likewise those bombs in the pockets, round and smooth enough to handle despite their corrugations, but at this juncture causing the temper to be anything

German farriers working on their horses in Grandcourt.

but smooth. Chafing one's skin they are, rubbing raw spots on one's tender skin; getting a wild Highland man into absolutely the best mood to make correct use of those same bombs when the time for action comes.

Here we are, at Mailly Maillet at last; somewhere about midnight, I should think, no lights being allowed even for the looking at watches — and no smoking either, though perhaps a little is going on surreptitiously, when the platoon officer's back is turned. So on through Mailly and out at its north end (this would be on the Serre road), wheel right, through a gate into a field, cross the field, and another, then — welcome command, "Form up in close column, and halt!" Every man loosens his equipment, and sits down where he has halted, weary and thankful to be rid of his load, for however short a space of that time which may be near to eternity.'

At Mailly make for Auchonvillers and from there to Hamel. Proceed along the road to Beaucourt, and from there towards Miraumont. After a couple of kilometres there will be a turning on the right for a very minor road to Grandcourt and beside it Baillescourt Farm, which has been rebuilt on the site of the old one. It was from here that it was feared that the German counter-attack would come in an attempt to wrest Beaucourt back from the Royal Naval Division. As you come in to Miraumont there is a sharp turning right which leads down to the site of the old mill. This was used as a German supply and munitions dump which blew up on 5th August 1916. In the middle of Miraumont there is a turning to the right to Pys, Courcelette and Petit Miraumont. Before taking it you may feel like visiting the grave of 2/Lt Uren, who is buried in the communal cemetery which is the turning to the left at the same point — the cemetery is at the end of the engagingly and accurately named Rue du Cimetiere. 2/Lt Uren was a casualty of the officers' patrol by 1/Lancashire Fusiliers on the 18th May 1916, described elsewhere, and was buried here by the Germans.

Once you have passed under the Railway Bridge turn right on the D151 to Grandcourt; some men from the Ulster Division actually made it to the edges of this village on July 1st, an extraordinary achievement. You can follow the road all the way back along to the tiny hamlet of St Pierre Divion, and you should emerge on Mill Road, the road between Thiepval and Hamel; alternatively you may cross the railway line at Beaucourt (or Beaumont) Station and take the more direct route back to Albert.

167

Map 13. Car tour behind the lines

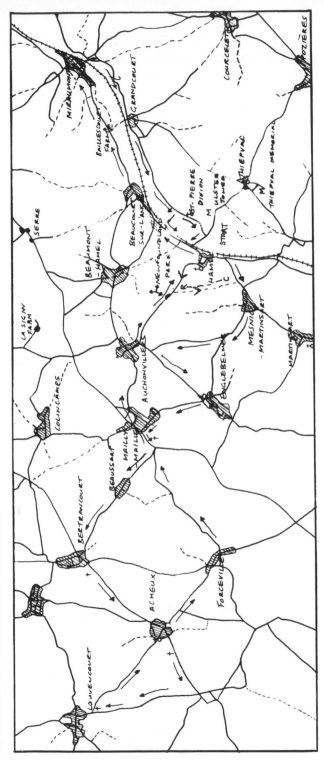

A CAR TOUR OF THE BEAUMONT HAMEL AND IMMEDIATE AREA BATTLEFIELD.

The car tour can be done very quickly — certainly within forty five minutes, if it is used purely to get one's bearings.

Assuming that the visitor is mobile, I would strongly recommend the car tour that is described below, which should enable the See Map 14 tourer to get a clearer idea of the ground which the guide describes; the walk is of greatest benefit, as it is very difficult to appreciate the detailed lie of the land until one has been over it by foot.

The car tour starting point is Hamel. Take the Auchonvillers road. The British were to the right of this road, the Germans obviously further over still. After some distance, Newfoundland Park will be seen on the right.

On reaching a T Junction, proceed into Auchonvillers by turning right. Remember that the French have a system of priority from the right; in this case you would have priority over oncoming traffic, but do be cautious. I tend to treat all road junctions where there might be some doubt about the right of way on the basis of coming to a halt, or very close to it.

Auchonvillers (Ocean Villas to the Tommy) was just behind the British line. At the crossroads in the village, turn right, and shortly afterwards left. This road used to be known as the Sunken Road,

The ruins of Beaumont Hamel, showing the road to Beaucourt, taken by a German photographer at the end of October 1916.

Frankfurt Trench Cemetery, with its excellent views across Newfoundland Park

and should not be confused with that nearer to Beaumont Hamel. Looking right you are viewing the support areas of the British line. A small road on your right is open only to those with business along it; this is Kilometre Lane; just below the turning, in descending order, was the crossing point of Sunken Road, of Fifth Avenue, a trench railway (installed after the July 1st attack) and Fourth Avenue.

The Sunken Road meets the main Mailly-Puisieux road, where you turn right. The farm at this junction is on the site of a sugar factory. On turning right, after à few yards, look across to your left across the fields to La Signy Farm. Staff Officers watched the battle for Serre on July 1st from there, and it was to this place that some tanks were brought up in the forlorn hope of being able to assist the November 13th attack in that area.

Looking across to the right provides a view of the British position before Beaumont Hamel. As the road curves around, the great mass of Serre Road Cemetery No 2 appears on the left. It is the largest British cemetery on the Somme, and stands in part of the old German Front Line. In due course, on the left, there is a small French Military Cemetery, soon followed by Serre Road Cemetery No I. Opposite the cemetery will be seen a small shrine chapel; take the right turning immediately beyond it — you are now on Frontier Lane, which ran for almost its entire length on or about the German Front Line. There are excellent views across the battlefield from here; the Thiepval Memorial stands out proudly, and nearer to Beaumont Hamel there are good views of Auchonvillers and the Hawthorn Crater.

Panorama of the German view from the eastern end of the Beaucourt Redoubt.

The Royal Naval Division Memorial, with the rebuilt and repositioned Beaucourt Church behind.

In Beaumont Hamel turn left and take the second on the left, the road inclining slightly up the ridge. This is Beaucourt Road. The cemetery sign to New Munich Trench is a good point to stop and look at the view which the Germans had over the British positions over on your right; whilst the strength of the Second German Line can also be appreciated.

Beaucourt Road brings one into Beaucourt; just before the ground starts dropping to the Ancre there is a crossroads: this is the area of the Beaucourt Redoubt. In Beaucourt turn right; at the edge of the village will be seen the Naval Division Memorial (in passing it is of interest to note that the Germans had a Marine Division in this sector in late June 1918). This road will bring you to Beaucourt Station, the scene of such heavy fighting in November 1916. Turn right here for Beaumont Hamel; this is Station Road. After some distance you will see a Quarry on the right which had dugouts and underground workings in it. Looking down into the valley on your left, just before Beaumont Hamel, you will see the Civil Cemetery; just before it is the eastern exit point of Y Ravine. Drive straight through Beaumont Hamel and come out on the New Beaumont Road, soon passing Beaumont Hamel Cemetery on your right and Hawthorn Crater above you on the left; Sunken Road is a hundred metres or so further on on the right. Some three hundred yards beyond this, on your left, is a well-established track, the bottom end of Old Beaumont Road. This is usually, except in severe weather conditions, passable, with care, to cars. Thus an alternative route is to go up this, and just when all looks as though it might be lost, a metalled surface makes its appearance on a left

Thiepval
Memorial

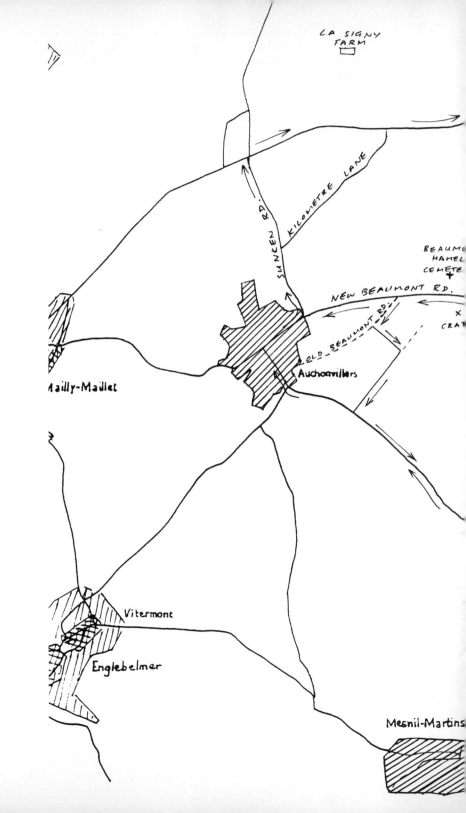

LA SIGNY FARM

SUNKEN RD.

KILOMETRE LANE

BEAUMO
HAMEL
CEMETE

NEW BEAUMONT RD.

OLD BEAUMONT RD.

Auchonvillers

X
CRAT

Mailly-Maillet

Vitermont

Englebelmer

Mesnil-Martins

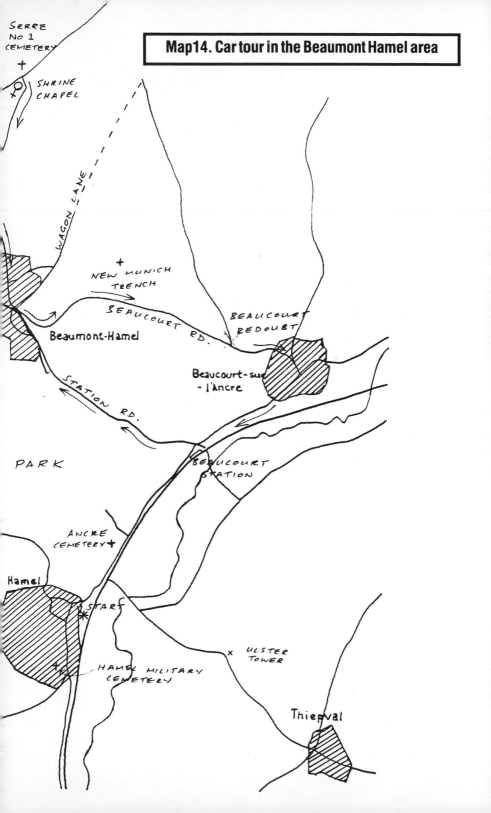

Map14. Car tour in the Beaumont Hamel area

SERRE
No 1
CEMETERY

SHRINE
CHAPEL

WAGON LANE

NEW MUNICH
TRENCH

BEAUCOURT RD.

BEAUCOURT
REDOUBT

Beaumont-Hamel

Beaucourt-sur
- l'Ancre

STATION RD.

PARK

BEAUCOURT
STATION

ANCRE
CEMETERY

Hamel

START

ULSTER
TOWER

HAMEL MILITARY
CEMETERY

Thiepval

The rather forlorn looking station at Beaucourt Hamel.

hand bend — do not attempt to follow the rest of Old Beaumont Road up to Auchonvillers! This metalled road brings you up to Hawthorn Ridge, again with good views, before bringing you out on the Hamel — Auchonvillers Road at the approximate location of Thurles Dump. Turn left, and you will be on the road to the Newfoundland Park and to Hamel. The **recommended** car route is to stay on the New Beaumont Road and return via Auchonvillers — it is safer for the car, if less interesting.

Beaumont Hamel civilian cemetery, in the same wartime location. The Quarry beyond, just above Station Road, was honeycombed with German dugouts.

A WALK ALONG THE FRONT.

The walk can take as long as a day if the tourer uses this as the basis on which he wishes to use the whole of the guide; or it can take about three hours of reasonably brisk movement. The time of the walk depends entirely on how the walker wishes to follow the options given.

It is possible to walk along tracks from the Ancre to the boundary of the 29th Division (July 1st) and 51st Division (13th November) attacks following the broad line of the front line on those momentous days. From the point of view of seeing the countryside, it is probably best to start from the Sunken Road, near the 1/8 Argylls' Memorial, because the countryside falls away as one comes

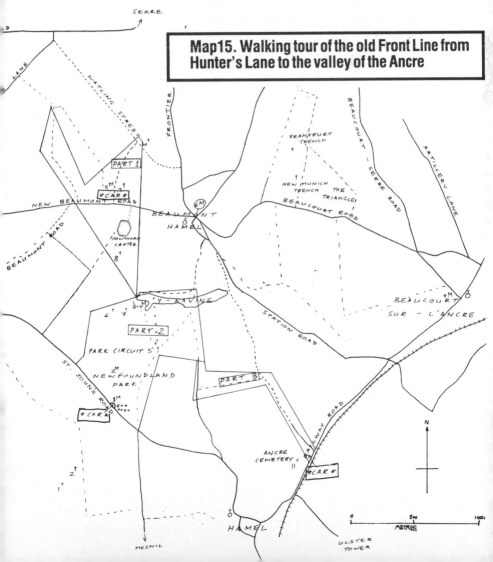

Map15. Walking tour of the old Front Line from Hunter's Lane to the valley of the Ancre

down into the Ancre valley, and so greater vistas are opened up as one walks along. It is also preferable to have two cars, so that one can be left at the end of the walk to bring the party back; the fit and hearty might well be willing to go both ways on foot! Stout walking shoes are recommended, and in most weather conditions these should suffice. It is also possible to take the walks in smaller sections, and cover the ground by a series of leapfrogs.

The route is indicated on the accompanying map; the relevant sections of the book which relate to what the walker should be seeing is stated alongside. For purposes of convenience I have split the route into parts, so that it can be taken as such or as a whole. Car parking points are indicated — the three best are by the Ancre Cemetery, the Newfoundland Memorial and the 1/8th Argylls' Memorial. Should the visitor have to go across a field, then please ensure that you keep to a field line and respect the local farmer's livelihood. The farmers of the region are very tolerant of the army of visitors that descend upon them, and it is in all our interests to follow basic country code practices. Be well aware that the countryside is still full of munitions and other battlefield debris; **the only safe rule is to leave it alone**. The French are great ones for shooting, and some times of the year there are many people out with their shotguns — one October visit sticks in my memory for the sheer number of guns out on the fields. So, again, be warned. If one parks a car other than the places I have suggested, do so with caution — tractors have a tendency to turn up at the most awkward time! One should be conscious of other road (and track) users.

Part 1: From the 1/8th Argyll's Memorial to Y Ravine.

Refer to Chapters 1, 2 (both in part), 3, 4, 5, 7 (in part), 8 (in part), 13 and 14.

The walk in this area is designed to enable the visitor to get a firm grasp of the ground over which the Lancashire Fusiliers on July 1st and the 8th Argylls on November 13th fought over. Leaving

Panorama from the slope of Redan Ridge, in No Man's Land.

German Front Line
1 July, 1916

Hawthorn
Crater

New
Beaumont
Road

the vehicle at the Memorial, walk up the Sunken Road right up to Redan Ridge Cemetery No 2. There are good views over the attacking ground, and beyond to Hawthorn Ridge. Along the Sunken Road, on the German side, there are signs in the banks of excavations of various types.

Returning to the Memorial, walk up to Beaumont Hamel Cemetery and beyond. Look back from the German position on the forward edge of the wood, to gain some impression of the task facing the British attackers. The Hawthorn Crater looms up above on the Ridge. Returning to the Memorial again take the track that runs alongside it to the west; this soon climbs out of an embankment and provides a good view of the British attack on the other side of the New Beaumont Road, as well as the exposed nature of the ground to the main British position on July 1st. The tunnel and communication trench opened up on the night preceding the July 1st attack ran across the track when it begins to level out with the adjacent fields.

Return to the Memorial and the road and walk back along it a few hundred yards towards Auchonvillers. Another track goes off on the right hand side of the road; this is Esau's Way. It is possible to drive along this, but I would not recommend it — a dent somewhere vital is a distinct possibility. I also very nearly ran over a shell last time I drove along here, so feet are perhaps best! The likely position of Malins when he filmed the Mine going off on Hawthorn Ridge is in some bushes towards the base of the embankment.

Esau's Way brings you around on Tenderloin Street and finally to White City. Even now that it is so much less high than it used to be (if stories of forty feet cliffs are to be taken at face value) it is obvious that this provided good cover from German observation, and made a logical place for Headquarters, Aid Posts and the like. It is possible to get to the site of the Bowery (meaning a plantation; the French name for this field is 'the cherry wood'), and which gave the British views into Beaumont Hamel itsel, only when there are no crops growing; it is now just part of a large field. The two east-west running embankments to the north of it mark the route

Old Beaumont Road   Auchonvillers Church   1/8 Argyll and Sutherland Highlanders Memorial   Sunken Road/Hunters Lane   The Remblai   Beaumont Hamel Military Cemetery

A view from the rear of the British line. White City was on the left of the bank which runs across the middle of the picture. The Bowery was off picture to the right of the bank on the right edge of the picture.

of Fourth Avenue (joining in this area with Third Avenue for a while) and Fifth Avenue. 88 Trench ran south from the Bowery and across the New Beaumont Road.

Return to the New Beaumont Road and walk up to the Hawthorn Crater, being extremely careful of the barbed wire fence that encloses the pathway. Look over what had been No Man's Land from its northern lip. Immediately to the east of the crater is the strong point that caused so much difficulty to the November 13 attack. Make one's way across the fields to the access road to Hawthorn Ridge Cemetery No 1 which is just in No Man's Land, a matter of metres in front of the old British Front Line. Again, important views are to be had. From the Cemetery make your way to the Newfoundland Park, entrance being made near the western end of Y Ravine.

Part 2: From Y Ravine to Mary Redan.

Refer to Chapters 1, 2 (both in part), 6, 7 (in part), 8 (in part), 13 (in part) and 14.

This is again a rather circuitous route, which takes the visitor around the Newfoundland Park. However, if the park has already been explored, or the visitor wishes to leave it for another time, omit the second section of this part of the walk. Should one wish to do the Park walk, read that section first and then return to what follows here.

Take the track leading eastwards, running along the northern edge of Y Ravine. There are good views of the ground behind Beaumont Hamel and the German positions that were there. Frankfurt Trench Cemetery may be seen, site of one of the furthest of the Highland Division's objectives on November 13th. After some five hundrd yards there is a track T Junction; go right (turning left will bring you out into Beaumont Hamel), down into Y Ravine

A view of Beaumont Hamel from the track running north of Y ravine.

and up a track on the other side of the ridge. Where the ground begins to rise is where the German Front Line crossed the track, the line following its course for a while before it snaked off to the south east. Y Ravine cemetery can be seen on your right; the German Front Line was about 150 yards to the north of it. The view that this part of the German front had over the attacking troops in what is now Newfoundland Park is excellent — even better if the trees did not obstruct the view. The ground on the right witnessed some of the heavy fighting of July 1st — the forlorn charge of 1/Essex for example. Mary Redan was more or less under the line of pylons that traverses the road, with the British line running west and south of it. After the abject failure of their attack on July 1st, the Newfoundland Regiment spent that night in support trenches some three hundred yards away, near to the track running down to Y Ravine Cemetery. On the left of the track is where the various battalions of the left hand Brigade of the 36th Ulster Division did their best on that fateful day.

If one moves a few yards off the track on the left hand side at the high point of ground, it is possible to look down into Beaucourt and to see the Naval Division memorial; you are looking across what would have been line after line of German defences.

View of Beaucourt from the Mary Redan area. The RND memorial is just visible to the right of the white buildings in the centre of the photograph.

Beaucourt   Royal Naval Division Memorial   Beaucourt Station

The western part of Y ravine, leading on to Point 89.

The Park Circuit.

Refer in particular to Chapters 6 and 7 (in part).

Having entered the Park at Y Ravine, make your way very carefully to the bottom of it, and proceed eastwards, observing the clear indentations and other signs of workings on its steep banks. Your route will be barred by barbed wire after a hundred and fifty yards or so; take the right fork, which is open to access. This is where heavy fighting took place between the German defenders and the attacking Highland Division in November. Following this branch of Y Ravine brings the visitor out to a well marked grass path and the German Front Line position, which ran east-west here along the length of the Ravine. Many of the British attackers on July 1st would have been walking past this position, heading eastwards, making them open to enfilade fire. Walk to Y Ravine Cemetery, then in No Man's Land. Over to the east, outside the park, the German line was some two to three hundred yards away, climbing up the ridge. Looking back to where you have just come from, and across to the German position, see how just exposed this attack was. Point 60 (the right boundary of the Newfoundland Regiment attack) is almost directly east of the cemetery, on the track running up to Mary Redan. The Caribou Memorial, sited on the extreme right of the Newfoundland attack is easily seen from the cemetery:

Trenches from which the 13 November attack by 7/Gordon Higlanders was probably launched.

thus some idea of the path of the mayhem that plunged the families of Newfoundland into mourning may be well appreciated.

Also in this direction may be seen the trench that runs diagonally across the park, close to the Danger Tree. This was the British Front Line trench on November 13th, when the axis of the advance of the attacking battalions was somewhat different, heading straight for the length of Y Ravine.

Proceed up the slope, but instead of heading straight for the Caribou, move to the south, and investigate some of the trench lines round the Superintendent's Lodge — these are much neglected by visitors. Then return to the Caribou and proceed along the grass path to the cemeteries and memorials clustered around the western edge of Y Ravine. Return to the path to Hawthorn Ridge Cemetery No 1, and then follow the route as above.

Part 3: From Mary Redan to the Ancre Cemetery

Refer to Chapters 1, 2 (both in part), 6 (in part), 9, 10, 11 (in part) and 14.

This section is very straightforward, but possibly rather muddy! About fifty yards or south of the pylons, a track leads off the road heading due east; at this point it was just outside the British Front.

Within a hundred and fifty yards or so the track crosses the German Front Line, which was heading in approximately a north-west, south east line. The track eventually meets another — to the left it will take you to Beaumont Hamel via the civil cemetery; to the right it leads down to Railway Road by Ancre British Cemetery. Within a few yards of this turning, the walker will be in the middle of the ground that formed part of the redoubt that was to cause so much trouble to the Naval Division, and which was finally crushed by the two tanks on November 14th.

The cross of sacrifice in the Ancre Cemetery in the centre of the photograph shows the deep dip which lay in No Man's Land on 1 July and was the jump off point for many men of the Royal Naval Division on 13 November. Taken from the road to Mary Redan.

RECOMMENDED READING

There are a number of guides on the Great War and on the Somme Battlefields. Foremost amongst the general guides remains Miss Rose Coombs, *Before Endeavours Fade*. This guide is reasonably priced and is an excellent book to lead the visitor around all the memorials and cemeteries, as well as the trench museums and other remnants of the war that exist on the Western Front. On the Somme there are several publications available. There is a straightforward and easy to use pocket guide, produced by Major and Mrs Holt; there is also a most useful accompanying map of the Somme battlefield as it is to-day, with the reverse showing dispositions during the battle. John Giles' *Somme Then and Now* is a useful anthology of explanation and individual experiences. It is profusely illustrated. Gerald Gliddon's *When the Barrage Lifts* is a very extensive topographical survey of the Somme area, with details on the villages and significant woods, trench lines and the like. It is occasionally factually flawed, but this should not detract too much from an enormous labour of love. There are frequent references to significant figures, such as war poets, VC winners and the like. The most recent entry to the lists is Martin and Mary Middlebrook's *The Somme Battlefields*. This is a first rate vade mecum to the Somme Department, and is an invaluable touring aid. It also makes interesting reading on its own! Whilst on Martin Middlebrook, his *First Day of the Somme* must still rate as one of the great books on that day, and of its type (a history illustrated by personal recollections) is, in my opinion, the best of its kind. Lyn MacDonald's *Somme* uses a broadly similar method, but covers the whole of the First Battle of the Somme, and is also an excellent read. These books are generally all available at the coffee and bookshop attached to the Delville Wood Museum.

BIBLIOGRAPHY

Tunnellers Capt W Grant Grieve and Bernard Newman. Herbert Jenkins 1936.

Official History France and Flanders 1916, Volumes 1 (Edmonds) *and 2* (Miles)

How I Filmed the War Lieutenant Geoffrey Malins OBE. Herbert Jenkins Ltd.

A Medico's Luck In the War Colonel David Rorie DSO. Milne and Hutchison 1929.

The Secret Battle AP Herbert. OUP 1982.

For the Sake of Example Anthony Babington. Leo Cooper 1983.

Shot at Dawn Julian Putkowski and Julian Sykes. Wharncliffe Publishing 1989.

From Trench and Turret SM Holloway. Royal Marines Museum

The HAC in the Great War ed G. Goold Walker. London, Seeley, Service and Co. 1930.

The Hawke Battalion: Some Personal Reminiscences of Four Years. Douglas Jerrold. Benn 1925.

The Royal Naval Division Douglas Jerrold. Hutchinson. 1923

Georgian Adventure Douglas Jerrold. William Collins Sons. 1937

General Lord Freyberg VC P Singleton-Gates Michael Joseph 1963

Bernard Freyberg VC. Soldier of Two Nations. Paul Freyberg. Hodder and Stoughton 1991.

What became of Corporal Pittman? Joy B Cave. Breakwater Books Ltd.

The Fighting Newfoundlander GWL Nicholson. Govt. of Newfoundland

I survived didn't I? The Great War Reminiscences of Private 'Ginger' Byrne. Ed and intro by Joy Cave. Leo Cooper 1993.

The Trail of the Caribou. Newfoundland in the First World War, 1914 — 18. T Murphy and P Kenney. Harry Cuff Publications Ltd.

My Bit. A Lancashire Fusilier at War 1914 — 1918 G. Ashurst ed. R Holmes. Crowood Press 1987

The History of the Lancashire Fusiliers 1914 — 1918 Vol 1. Major General JC Latter. Gale and Polden 1949.

The Cross of Sacrifice, Vol 1 SD and DB Jarvis. Robert Medals Pub 1993.

The Tanks Volume 1 1914 — 1939. BH Liddell Hart. Cassell 1959.

The Somme AH Farrar-Hockley. Batsford 1964.

Somme Lyn Macdonald. Michael Joseph 1983

The First Day of the Somme. Martin Middlebrook. Allen Lane 1971

History of the 36th (Ulster) Division. Cyril Falls. McGaw, Stevenson and Orr Ltd 1922.

History of 51st (Highland) Division. W Bewsher, DSO, MC. Wm Blackwood & Sons 1921.

A History of the Black Watch in the Great War. Volume Two, Territorial Force Maj Gen AG Wauchope CB. Medici Society 1926.

History of the 17th (Northern) Division. A Hilliard Atteridge. R McElhose & Co 1929.

The East Yorkshire Regiment in the Great War. Everard Wyrall. Harrison and Sons 1928

History of the Dorsetshire Regiment, 1914 — 1919. Henry Ling. 1932

The Sixth Gordons in France and Flanders. D MacKenzie, MC. Rosemount, Aberdeen 1922

Marshal Foch walking through Newfoundland Park on the occasion of the unveiling of the 51 Division Memorial.

INDEX

Abbeville, 108
Abbott, Ptes George & Stanley, 71
Acheux, 34, 146, 162
Acheux Wood, 47, 141
Agincourt, Battle of, 7
Albert, 23, 67, 150
Amiens, 139
Ancre, River, 7, 19, 20, 23, 101, 106, 107, 110, 117, 119, 122, 128, 129, 130, 139
Arras, 36
Anderson, 2/Lt A.F.D., 48
Ashurst, George, 36-38, 40, 44-47
Asquith, A.M., 121
Auchonvillers, 47, 48, 55, 65, 73, 94, 95, 100, 102, 103, 129, 156, 167
Authie, 164
Ayre, 2/Lt G & W, Capts E & B, 71, 148

Babington, Judge Anthony, 133
Baillescourt Farm, 113, 167
Baly, Lt, 92
Battles:
    Advance to Victory, 146
    Ancre, 23-24, 75-132 passim, 135, 136
    Arras, 45, 87
    Flers-Courcelette, 23, 128
    Loos, 58
    Ludendorff Offensive, 139
    Somme, passim
Beaucourt, 106, 111, 113, 117, 118, 120, 124, 130, 131
Beaucourt Mill, 118
Beaucourt Redoubt, 23, 106, 120, 121, 170
Beaucourt Road, 20, 55, 60, 76, 127, 131
Beacourt [Hamel] Station, 19, 106, 116, 119
Beaumont Hamel, passim
Beaumont Road (New), 31, 34, 43, 46, 52, 76
Beaumont Road (Old), 70, 76, 171, 177
Beausart, 129, 162
Begg, Capt. H., 103
Bertrancourt, 162
Birmingham, 150
Bluff, The, 26
Booth, Lt Col, 82
Bottomley, Horatio, 135
Boulogne, 101

Bowery, The, 33, 77, 177
Bradford, Brig Gen 'Boy', VC, 126
British and Dominion Armies
    1/8 Argylls, 83-95 passim, 164-167
    7/Argylls, 83-95
    4/Bedfords, 148
    6/Black Watch, 75, 76, 81, 82
    1/Borderers, 22, 58, 60, 150
    Cape Mounted Rifles, 154
    Collingwood Bn, 107
    1/Royal Dublin Fusiliers, 21
    1/Dorsets, 154
    6/Dorsets, 141, 162
    Drake Bn, 107
    7/East Yorks, 141-148 passim
    1/Essex, 22, 55, 61, 62, 63, 65, 66
    Forestry Corps (Newfoundland), 57
    2/Royal Fusiliers, 21,29, 45, 51
    4/Gordons, 82
    5/Gordons, 82
    6/Gordons, 85, 88, 95-96
    7/Gordons, 75, 76, 81, 82, 181
    HAC (Honourable Artillery Company), 113, 117-120
    1/Hampshires, 154
    2/Hampshires, 22, 57, 65, 66
    Hawke Bn, 107, 109, 111, 114, 115, 136, 155
    2/HLI, 85, 88, 92
    Hood Bn, 107, 117, 121, 122, 123, 126, 164
    Howe Bn, 117
    1/Royal Inniskilling Fusiliers, 21
    9/Irish Fusiliers, 21
    12/Irish Rifles, 21
    1/King's Own Scottish Borderers, 22
    1/Lancashire Fusiliers, 21, 33-48 passim, 52, 162, 167, 176
    London Scottish, 40
    R.M.L.I. (Royal Marine Light Infantry), 107
    2/RMLI, 115,116
    1/RMLI, 115
    16/Middlesex, 21, 29, 153
    Nelson Bn, 107, 115, 135, 136
    Newfoundland Regiment, 7, 22, 55-74 passim, 126, 148, 163, 164
    8/Norfolks, 71
    Ox and Bucks L.I., 92
    4/Seaforths, 76
    5/Seaforths, 81, 85, 89
    6/Seaforths, 85, 93
    2/South Wales Borderers, 21, 34, 58, 60, 148, 151